D1219997

ILLINOIS PRAIRIE DPL

WHITETAIL HUNTING

SHAWN PERICH &
MICHAEL FURTMAN

ILLINOIS PRAIRIE DISTRICT LIBRARY

CREATIVE
PUBLISHING
international

CHANHASSEN, MINNESOTA

www.creativepub.com

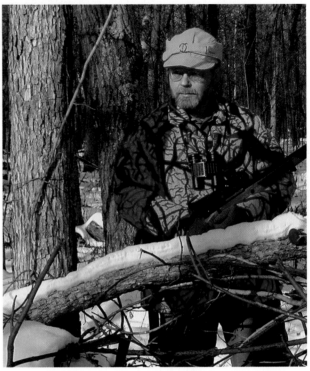

SHAWN PERICH is an avid hunter and angler. His outdoor and conservation articles and columns have appeared in numerous magazines and newspapers. Shawn has authored many books, including *Backroads of Minnesota, Fly-Fishing the North Country* and *Fishing Lake Superior.* He lives in northern Minnesota, along the Lake Superior shoreline.

MICHAEL FURTMAN has authored more than a dozen books on hunting and fishing, including *Duck Country, Black Bear Country, Whitetail: Phantom of the Forest* and *Trout Country.* His photography and outdoor articles have appeared in hundreds of regional and national magazines. Michael lives in northern Minnesota.

Copyright © 2004 by Creative Publishing international, Inc.
18705 Lake Drive East
Chanhassen, MN 55317
1-800-328-3895
www.creativepub.com

All rights reserved.

President/CEO: Michael Eleftheriou

Vice President/Publisher: Linda Ball

Vice President/Retail Sales & Marketing: Kevin Haas

Executive Editor, Outdoor Group: Barbara Harold

Creative Director: Brad Springer

Project Manager: Tracy Stanley

Photo Editor: Angela Hartwell

Director, Production Services: Kim Gerber

Production Manager: Helga Thielen

Production Staff: Laura Hokkanen, Stephanie Barakos

Printed on American paper by: R. R. Donnelley

10 9 8 7 6 5 4 3 2 1

WHITETAIL HUNTING
by Shawn Perich & Michael Furtman

Cover Photo by: John R. Ford

Contributing Photographers: Charles J. Alsheimer, Mike Barlow, Dominique Braud/Dembinsky Photo Associates, Denver Bryan, John R. Ford, Michael H. Francis, Brad & Carol Herndon, Tes Randle Jolly, Donald M. Jones, Bill Kinney, Lon E. Lauber, Bill Lea, Stephen W. Maas, Bill Marchel, Mark Raycroft

Contributing Manufacturers: Barrie Archery, LLC; Browning; Cabela's, Inc.; Carl Zeiss Sports Optics; Gerber Legendary Blades; HHA Sports; Hunter's Specialties; Primos Hunting Calls, Inc.; Scent-Lok; Sightron, Inc.; Tink's.

ISBN 1-58923-129-5

Library of Congress information on file

799.2
PER
c)

WHITETAIL HUNTING

CONTENTS

The Whitetail Era

The white-tailed deer is America's most popular big game animal. Remarkably adaptable, it survives—and often thrives—in northern forests, midwestern farmlands, southern swamps, western scrub and even suburban backyards. Wherever it is found, the whitetail is an elusive quarry that challenges even the most experienced hunters. You can spend a lifetime honing your deer hunting skills, and many hunters do just that.

Today's deer hunting is better than it's ever been before. In recent decades, scientific wildlife management has greatly increased both the range and abundance of whitetails, providing close-to-home hunting opportunities for millions of hunters. This truly is the Whitetail Era, a golden age for growing numbers of devoted deer hunters.

But there can be too much of a good thing. Without predation or adequate hunter harvest, whitetails proliferate to nuisance levels. Hungry deer destroy vegetation in farm fields, forests, and backyards. Human health risks, from car-deer collisions to Lyme disease, increase when deer are overabundant. Recent discoveries of chronic wasting disease (CWD) in wild deer populations may indicate that high deer densities can lead to starvation, winter loss and disease.

Wildlife managers use regulated hunting to keep deer populations in check. Extra antlerless-only permits, special hunts and extended seasons are used as incentives to encourage hunters to kill more deer. Many hunters are aware of their individual role in deer management. They practice local management by selectively harvesting deer to maintain a balanced herd.

Deer hunting has become more sophisticated during the Whitetail Era, but the basic challenge remains the same. The white-tailed deer is a wary animal that relies on a keen sense of smell, excellent hearing, and eyesight to detect and avoid danger. To beat a deer's sensory defenses, you must stay quiet, be patient and keep the wind in your face. Within these ground rules, you have many ways to play the game. Traditional tactics—driving, standing and still-hunting—are effective wherever whitetails roam. Newer strategies—calling, scents, rattling and decoys—have entered the hunting mainstream.

While firearms seasons are the most popular, archery and "black powder" hunts attract hunters who enjoy longer seasons and less hunting pressure. Many hunters take up bowhunting or muzzleloading so they can enjoy the challenge of these methods and spend more time afield. Archers are frequently used by wildlife managers to harvest deer in suburban situations. In some metropolitan areas, experienced bowhunters have formed organizations that specialize in safe removal of problem deer.

For many hunters, however, deer hunting is simply an enjoyable time spent outdoors with family and friends. You don't need to be an expert hunter to have fun. How do you get started in deer hunting? A good beginning is to read this book. We've supplied you with the basic information you need to understand whitetail behavior, find a place to hunt, select the right equipment and choose a proven hunting strategy. What you learn in the following pages will give you the confidence necessary to become a successful hunter.

Your enjoyment of whitetail hunting doesn't have to end when the season closes. There are many ways to extend it.

For example, successful hunters bring home venison, a lean, mild-flavored meat you can prepare in many ways. You can visit your hunting area in winter and early spring to scout, learn more about deer and look for shed antlers. Attend hunting shows and seminars. Get involved in a hunting or conservation organization.

When you step into the world of the whitetail, hunting becomes a way of life!

CHAPTER ONE

World of the Whitetail

No hunter succeeds without complete knowledge of the animal he or she pursues.

If that's true, then it is doubly true for the deer hunter, for the white-tailed deer is a complex animal, physically and behaviorally. You simply can't get close enough to one of these secretive animals without knowing how it behaves, and why it does so.

As with all animals, two primary urges control the whitetail's behavior. Food is first, for without that, there is no health. Sex is second, for once adequate food is acquired, the majority of a healthy, well-fed whitetail's behavior revolves around reproduction.

Not just the actual sex act, mind you, but the whole cycle of reproducing. For the buck, that means acquiring the size and antler configuration to "out compete" his rivals and to attract does.

For the doe, it means being healthy enough to carry a fetus through the long winter, to give birth in spring and to ensure her fawns grow large enough to survive their first winter.

Ensuring success in these energy-intensive endeavors requires physical skills and finely tuned senses. Whitetails have all of that, the result of eons of evolution, during which they've been repeatedly tested by weather, predators and disease. The weak were found lacking, and the strong were not. The hunter must pit himself or herself against the result of natural selection over thousands of generations—quite a daunting task.

Deer Anatomy

It may seem strange to begin a discussion on the whitetail's physiology by looking first at its stomach, but it really is the stomach that in many ways influences the shape of everything else.

Digestive System

So how does a stomach influence a species? Consider this: If a deer must stand long enough in one spot to thoroughly chew its food until it is digestible, it also exposes itself to predators for long periods. The whitetail's compound stomach is comprised of four chambers: rumen, reticulum, omasum and abomasum. When it has consumed a sufficient quantity of food, it travels to a secure hiding area, brings the food back up, and chews its cud in relative leisure and safety. By being able to digest and chew food at a later time, a deer can browse and move, making it a more difficult target to find.

The white-tailed deer selectively chooses more digestible plants, or the most digestible parts of plants, rather than consuming large quantities of less-digestible food. Deer rarely stand in one place for long, but prefer to nip and move. Once they've temporarily eaten their fill and stored the food in the rumen (the stomach's first chamber), white-tailed deer move to an area in their territory they consider safe. Here they bed down, and once they are confident that no danger awaits them, they regurgitate a ball, or bolus, of food for further chewing.

Fall is a transition time for whitetails – from the low-stress of summer to the high energy of the rut.

White-tailed deer have a highly specialized digestive system that permits both this feeding behavior and the ability to eat a variety of plant foods. Although they are, like cattle, considered ruminants, they are not true grazers as are cows. Cattle can eat grass or other ruffage. This involves considerable "head down" grazing in order to consume the large volume of less-nutritious forage needed. A cow or bison with its head down all the time isn't being particularly alert to threats. Herding behavior offsets this because as some animals graze, others stand by, chewing their cuds, and act as guards.

Whitetails can afford to be selective; the forest and its edge hold a wide variety of succulent plants, browse, fruits and nuts. True grazers, like cattle and bison, are animals of the plains where they feed on varieties of less-nutritious and less-digestible grasses.

The fact that deer can be choosy means they have a slightly different digestive system than other ruminants. The whitetails' rumen is smaller than that of other deer, and their salivary glands are larger.

After carefully selecting their food, whitetails nip it from the main plant. Whitetails lack incisors on the upper jaw (and have no true canine teeth), so they shred food from the plant stem by grasping it between the lower incisors and the tough, bony roof of the upper jaw. If you study browsed plants carefully, you'll soon be able to distinguish those slightly shredded twig tips left by browsing whitetails from the cleanly cut tips made by other animals, like rabbits.

The whitetail's selective feeding behavior is aided by its nimble lips and narrow face, which have evolved to allow them to "insert" their face and mouth into trees and shrubs, or among various ground plants, to select not only the species of choice, but the portion of the plant they desire. After tearing off a mouthful, whitetails chew the food very briefly—only enough to swallow it—which is aided by the abundance of saliva whitetails can manufacture.

A deer skull (above). Due to their sophisticated digestive system, whitetails are able to eat a variety of foods— acorns (right), corn (below).

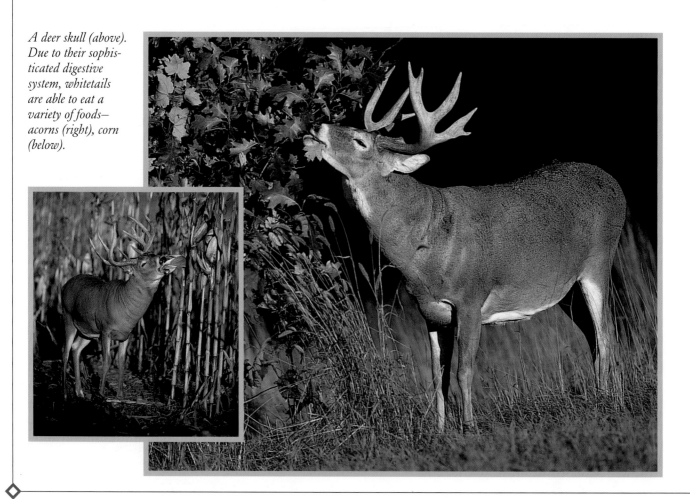

Then, as stated earlier, they move off to their bedding area to further chew and digest their food.

Knowing where deer bed, then, is an important bit of knowledge for the hunter. Deer repeatedly use the same bedding areas, and routes to them. Once bedded, they are nearly impossible to find, so the hunter's best chance is to waylay the deer on its way from a feeding area to the bedding grounds.

With its stomach dictating that it be fed, almost everything else about the deer's body is designed to facilitate that. Feet, legs, joints, bones; all are designed to get a deer quietly around the forest so that it can find the food its stomach demands, and to get it out of trouble should trouble find it. Its fine array of senses evolved to provide it with an early-warning system, and to utilize the chemical messages left by its glandular system.

Speed and stealth for whitetails begin "where the rubber meets the road"–in their case where the keratin meets the detritus (OK–in lay terms, where the outer hoof meets the decaying material that makes up the Earth).

Hooves and Legs

The whitetail's narrow, tapered hooves are specialized to allow minimal contact with the ground. That serves deer well in two ways: Minimal contact reduces friction, which increases speed; and narrow hooves are easier to place quietly amidst the forest floor's noisy leaves and sticks. In addition, whitetails are "perfect walkers," which simply means that while walking at normal speed, the rear hooves fall exactly into the tracks of the front hooves. The advantage of this seems fairly obvious: Once the front hooves have been safely and quietly placed, the deer knows that its rear steps will be equally well placed.

Dew-claws

The track of a whitetail hoof is like that of paired commas. Looking at a whitetail's tracks, one would easily assume that it only has two toes per leg. If you guessed that, you'd be exactly half right, since there are two other vestigial toes

Dewclaws are easy to identify (above). Deer usually retire to a secluded location to bed and further chew their food (left).

farther up the back of the leg, known as dewclaws. The front legs' dewclaws are nearer to the hoof than those of the rear. Usually dewclaws don't show in tracks unless the deer has been walking in snow or mud, or running at high speed.

When walking, the closed, rounded point of the track faces forward. However, at full gallop, or braking down a steep embankment, deer splay their hooves wide at the front, reversing the impression. Since whitetails carry more weight on their front hooves, these are slightly larger than those of the rear, and the hooves of bucks are larger than those of same-age does. Some research indicates that buck hooves are slightly more rounded at the tip than those of does, perhaps because the extra weight carried by mature bucks causes additional wear. Some also believe,

although studies have never proven it, that drag marks appearing between tracks in snow less than 6 inches in depth indicate the passing of a buck. In snow deeper than 6 inches, however, it is impossible for deer not to leave drag marks, so their presence reveals little about age or sex.

The hoof itself is comprised of the outer, tough horn made of keratin (our fingernails are made of the same material) and a spongy surface on the sole that provides some shock absorption and traction. Deer hooves wear constantly and, like our own nails, are replaced as they wear, although the rate of growth varies with the season.

Their narrow feet and legs are designed for speed and maneuverability. The rear legs provide the greatest thrust, while the front legs steer with great precision. Unlike humans, the whitetail's front shoulders lack a collarbone assembly

A whitetail track can tell the hunter many things— including speed and direction of travel (above). At full run, in the open, deer have been clocked galloping at speeds of nearly 40 mph (left). Agile and quick, whitetails have several options for escaping predators. One that is often used and very effective is leaping fences (below).

and are free-floating–their front legs can pivot independently of each other, allowing for those "on the dime" turns at which we marvel.

A powerful rear leg structure allows whitetails to leap over tall obstructions, even from a standing start. From a dead stop, they can clear a fence or windfall of up to 7 feet; once running, that vertical height increases to over 8 feet.

Coat

Bundling all this together is a mass of muscle and a coat of dense, hollow hair–not fur. The whitetail's coat is a shade of color that blends in well with many surroundings. That the darkest hair is on the top, especially along the spine, is no accident. It gives the impression of a shadow cast from above. Grayish hairs scattered through the winter coat's shoulders and haunches also tend to act as a shadow effect, as well as serving to blend into the

trunks of trees. White patches beneath the chin and along the entire underside help to break up the deer's own natural shadow, making it look less than three dimensional to passing predators.

But beyond just camouflage, the whitetail's coat is designed to protect. Since it must do so both in warm weather and extreme cold, whitetails evolved two specialized coats and therefore must molt twice a year. The spring molt occurs in May in the North, and as early as March in Texas and is marked by the shedding of the long winter hair. Winter coats are usually fully grown-in by mating season.

Their winter coat, the one most hunters encounter, is comprised of darker, sun-absorbing guard hairs and a second layer of woolly underfur. Unlike the summer coat, the winter coat's individual guard hairs are hollow, increasing the amount of dead air space and insulation. So little heat escapes that snow falling on a deer doesn't melt.

In summer, a deer's coat looks smooth and is reddish brown (right). In winter the hair turns grayish and becomes duller, as well as more shaggy looking (below).

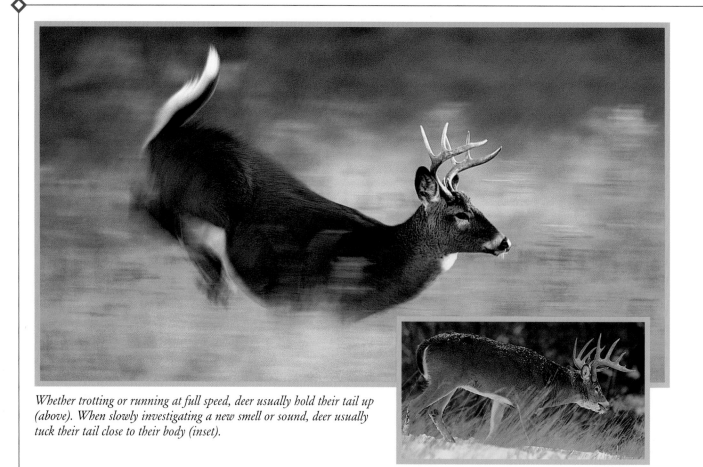

Whether trotting or running at full speed, deer usually hold their tail up (above). When slowly investigating a new smell or sound, deer usually tuck their tail close to their body (inset).

Tail

Considering that whitetails have evolved a coat that—besides keeping them protected from the elements—is designed to "protect" them from predators through camouflage, one might wonder why they have such a conspicuous white tail for which they are named.

This "flag" serves an important purpose. Its evolution was no accident. Although deer survival depends largely upon being unseen in the forest, they are social animals that need to keep track of each other. Thus they evolved a tail that meets both needs.

When lowered, the tail presents only minimal white to the searching eyes of a predator, and so doesn't adversely impact camouflage. Raised, however, it becomes a white beacon to other deer, serving as a warning that danger is present, allowing fleeing deer to easily follow each other. Since the tail is raised only when danger is imminent, and only when the whitetail is exercising its speed and agility in an escape (which are its last, best defense), it is probably no disadvantage that predators can also see the flag. However, whitetails don't always raise this flag when escaping. A deer that is trying to sneak away often pins its tail tightly to its rump.

The tail also serves as a silent early-warning system. When a whitetail is suspicious of a noise or object, it erects its rump hair and pumps its tail up and down. Since deer usually turn to face the possible threat, this silent warning is usually only viewed by other deer to its rear. Once the danger is identified and located, the tail becomes fully erect. Now every deer within eyesight is silently warned. If the noise or intruder is eventually deemed to be non-threatening, the cautious whitetail will flick its tail side-to-side once, relax, and go on about its business. This flick lets other deer know that the "coast is clear."

This is often the hunter's view after startling and jumping bedded or feeding deer.

Senses

When you live life as food for something else, much of what you do is designed to avoid ending up on something else's menu while you find something to put on yours. To that end, white-tailed deer have evolved remarkably acute senses.

Smell

The whitetail's sense of smell may just be the most important when it comes to avoiding predators and communicating with other deer. Although studies have never quantified just how much better the whitetail's sense of smell is than our own, there is unanimous agreement among scientists and hunters that it far outstrips our own meager scenting abilities. Not only can deer differentiate between species through just the use of scent (even the best of us would have a hard time scenting a wolf, but even if we did catch a whiff, would you know what it is you're smelling?), they seem to be able to determine the age of an odor. In other words, wolf scent that is old, though it registers on the deer's "smell-o-meter," causes a far different behavioral reaction than one that is fresh.

When it comes to warning deer of danger, the sense of smell is the ultimate judge. Hearing a noise, the deer will look in that direction. Seeing what is making that noise may cause the deer to stare intently. But even when taken together, the deer still may not be able to identify the intruder or be inclined to flee. One good whiff, however, is enough to finally pass judgment. And, of course, a deer needn't see a human, wolf or cougar to know that it needs to disappear. Seeing a predator simply isn't required when you can smell it.

Scent is also an important communication tool, especially for fawns and does trying to keep track of each other, as a means of finding a prospective mate, and for detecting invisible, chemical sign-posts that tell bucks about each other's rank and territory. And as mentioned earlier, deer can scent-track each other, a useful tool in following other deer to safety or food.

Finally, like us, deer follow their noses to food.

Whitetails do one thing that especially enhances their sense of smell. They wet their nose with their tongue so that scent molecules increase in dampness as they enter the nostrils. Molecules so humidified tend to cling better to olfactory cells.

It makes great evolutionary sense that an animal that lives in the woods, where the distance one can see is limited, would develop other means of interpreting signals. The sense of smell fills that role. But deer have at least one other tool that aides them when visibility is limited—an acute sense of hearing.

A whitetail that has detected the odor of a predator stares in the direction the odor came from to pick up any movement.

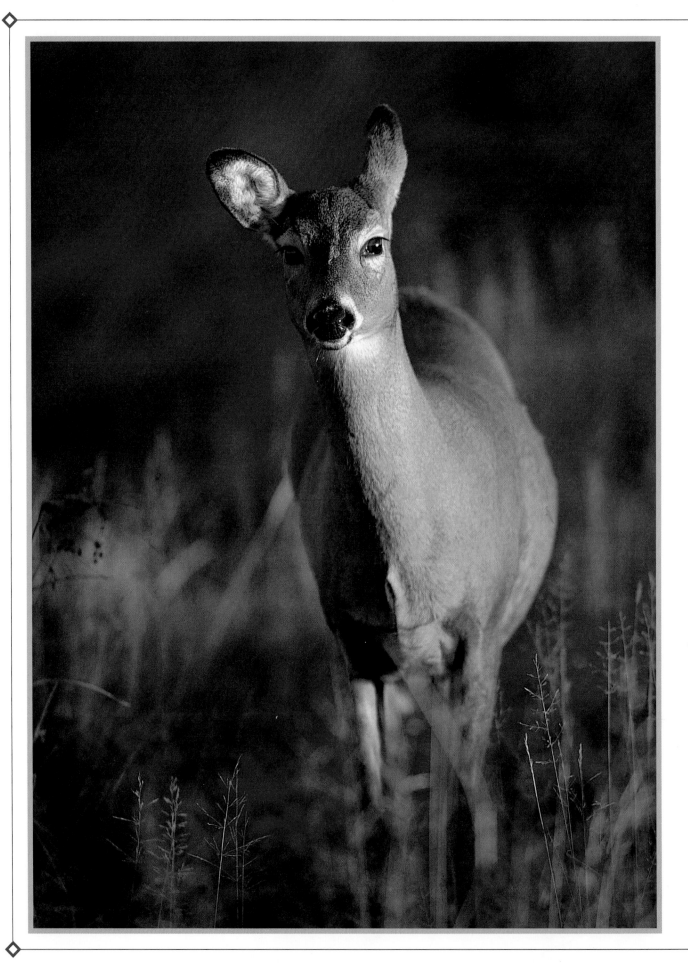

Hearing

You and I have eyesight that perceives depth of field, or distance. Our hearing, however, does not, built as we are with immobile ears set on either side of our head. The whitetail's ears sit atop the head, and can move independently of each other. It isn't uncommon to see a deer with one of these large "audible scoops" facing one direction, with the other pointing off somewhere else. Whitetails may even keep one ear forward and another rearward while at full gallop, so that they might hear if they're being pursued from behind, while they simultaneously listen for trouble ahead. By being able to direct their ears, whitetails not only hear better than we do, they can determine the direction and distance from which a sound emanates. If it reaches the left ear first, then whatever made the sound is nearer to that side, and through comparing the minute difference in time it takes the sound to reach the other ear, deer can effectively triangulate to get a fix on the source.

While humans tend to turn toward a sound, deer may just turn an ear toward it. By doing so, they can amplify the noise. For gathering sound waves, whitetails have four times more ear surface area than do humans. In addition, they can hear sounds that we can't, particularly at the higher frequencies. White-tailed deer can hear sounds in the 20 to 20,000 Hertz range; humans, from 500 to 12,000 Hz. The deer's hearing isn't supreme in the animal world, though. Dogs can hear better, being able to discern sounds in a range that begins lower (15 Hz) and ends higher (44,000 Hz).

Despite excellent hearing, sudden loud noises may confuse the whitetail's ability to detect the source or direction of the sound. As some hunters can attest, deer sometimes stand around even after a loud gunshot, apparently unable to find the source. Most research indicates that deer move around less, or are more nervous, on windy days, most likely because they are uncomfortable with their diminished hearing.

Vision

The third major sense, vision, is the whitetail's least acute. It isn't that their eyesight is poor. It just isn't quite as superb as are their hearing and scenting abilities.

White-tailed deer eyes are adapted to see well both in low light (even in darkness) as well as under the bright light of day. Their pupils contract into a narrow slit, unlike ours, which form a circular opening. This slit concentrates light in a narrow band against

Not only do deer have a wider radius of vision than humans (deer field of vision in red – human in yellow), their pupils gather about nine times more light than human eyes. Deer also have better peripheral vision.

Deer can pinpoint the source of a sound hundreds of yards away, particularly low frequencies, such as other deer grunting.

the back of the eye, or retina, which contains the light-sensing receptors clustered in a horizontal band. Combined with the actual placement in the skull, deer have a remarkable 270-degree field of view. The only place they can't see is behind them. Our field of view is limited to 180 degrees.

Inside their eye, whitetails (and other animals designed to see in low light) have a membrane that you and I lack–the tapetum lucidum. It is this membrane that reflects the light of your car's headlights. It also allows light to reflect through their eye's light receptors twice, increasing their ability to see in the dark.

Do whitetails see color? That debate still rages. In order to see color as we know it, an animal must have the right kind of photoreceptors. Our eyes have two kinds; cones, which give us daylight and color vision, and rods, which enable vision in low light, but in shades of gray, like a black-and-white movie. Deer definitely have rods, but studies conflict on whether or not they have cones. Two studies insist that there are cones on the whitetail's retina, and seem to indicate that whitetails see some color, especially in the yellow and blue ranges. These studies also indicate that if deer do see color, they are least sensitive to long wavelengths–those in the red-orange range. However, another study that

used electron microscopes found that whitetails do not have color-sensing cones. Some studies also indicate that whitetails see well in the ultraviolet range, which is invisible to humans.

Whatever the case, deer are remarkably adept at seeing motion. The slightest movement by a hunter or other whitetail will focus the deer's unwavering attention. Deer can stand unblinking for what seems like an eternity, trying to get you to move again. Often they'll lower their head for a second, trying to fool you into thinking that they are no longer observing you. Within seconds, however, they snap their head back up. If you've moved so much as an inch, they'll note the difference and vanish in a flurry of bounds and snorts.

The whitetail's array of senses is imposing. It is very difficult for any living thing to sneak up on them, although obviously this occurs or predators would have vanished long ago, and human hunters would have long since given up. And although we've discussed their senses separately, they work in concert. A deer may hear a sound first, then turn to watch for movement. If it can't see it, it may move downwind to see if it can catch a whiff. One or another of the senses will eventually determine whether or not the deer can remain safely, or warn it to move off.

Predators, such as wolves, are able to beat a deer's acute senses often enough to keep the pack alive and well fed.

Communication

Whitetails spend most of their lives in groups, a habit that improves their chances of survival. With many eyes and ears on alert, the deer can easily detect an approaching intruder. When one deer senses trouble, it quickly communicates alarm to other group members. Understanding how whitetails communicate can help you predict their behavior—upping your odds of taking a deer.

Sounds Made by Deer

Compared to other animals, white-tailed deer aren't particularly vocal. That shouldn't be surprising, since sound doesn't carry well in the woods, and animals that are prey species are better off not advertising their presence by making a lot of noise.

That said, whitetails do make an array of sounds, all of which are designed to communicate with each other. Sounds are made by both sexes and at all ages.

Of course, females and fawns regularly communicate through a series of grunts, whines and bleats. Doe-fawn calls are seldom useful to hunters, although a fawn bleat or bawl can sometimes lure a doe into view.

Of most importance to hunters are the sounds deer make during the autumn mating season. Both bucks and does emit agonistic calls—sounds designed to imply aggressiveness. A single low grunt is used by both sexes year-round to let other deer know that they aren't at all happy about sharing food, or that the other deer is too near or unwelcome. As the encounter becomes more intense, the aggressor deer may add a series of snorts. This "grunt-snort" call is most fully developed in rutting bucks, particularly between mature bucks that are of near-equal stature physically and socially. The most threatening sound a rutting, dominant buck can make is the "grunt-snort-wheeze" designed to let his rival know that he won't tolerate his presence. If the competitor doesn't respond to this call by leaving, a dominance battle may erupt.

Although not often heard by hunters, another whitetail call made during the autumn, especially during the rut, is the "tending grunt." This low, guttural sound is emitted by a buck courting a doe in heat, or while he is tracking her.

Some hunters confuse this mating grunting with the whitetail's alarm call. Often called a "buck snort" this wheezing whistle is actually made by both bucks and does. Caused by the sudden

Bucks emit a variety of grunt sounds during the rut. Distinguishing between them is challenging, and hunters find that volume and intensity vary depending on the situation.

expelling of air through the nasal passage, it serves as a warning to all other deer nearby that danger lurks. When deer are suddenly startled, this sound is singular and explosive; when they have detected trouble from a distance, warning is often given in a series of lengthier snorts.

Body Language

Sometimes just a barely perceptible movement of an ear is all a deer needs to communicate. Other times it's just a twitch of a muscle—and danger is understood.

Deer in groups may stomp their feet when alarmed to warn others. But foot-stomping can be heard for only a short distance.

Although not a widely used warning system, deer stomping their feet is effective enough to be used occasionally.

The most-used communication tool may be a deer's tail. A casual side-to-side motion—wagging similar to that of horses or cattle—with no hair standing erect signals no danger. If the tail begins a sharp side-to-side motion with the tail horizontal or upright and hairs are erect, you know that the deer is sending out signals of mild alarm. If nothing else confirms that feeling, the deer may go back to what it was doing and not take flight. But once the deer is convinced the danger is real, it will hold the tail upright, waving it back and forth, exposing the white hair underneath. This signals a high state of alarm, and any deer within sight of it will quickly leave the area.

Other Silent Messages

Glands—those mysterious chemical-producing organs found in the oddest of locations—exert tremendous control over the seasonal routine of the whitetail.

Located primarily in, or just below, the skin, glands serve as generators of chemical communication for whitetails, enhancing the role of the deer's already important sense of smell. Each gland emits its own unique scent, known as a "pheromone." Think of pheromones as the alphabet of an olfactory language, a language that allows deer to tell each other things about their readiness to mate, to recognize each other, to establish dominance or territory, and to warn others of impending danger. All of these important signals are transmitted without a sound, and are readable by passing deer long after the messenger has disappeared. In a forest environment, where sound carries poorly and members of the species rarely congregate in large numbers, an eloquent language of odors seems like an immense advantage. It is.

The roles of some glands aren't fully understood because they have only recently been discovered. However, we do know, or suspect, that the following glands function in certain ways.

• Found just in front of the eye, the *preorbital gland* is a hairless, shallow slit-like pocket. Witnessing a deer scent-mark a twig with this gland brings on an involuntary twinge in the human observer, for it almost appears that the deer is poking a stick into its eye. Bucks frequently rub the preorbital gland on twigs that overhang buck scrapes. Researchers don't know what message is conveyed by the scent emitted from this gland, but it certainly is of importance to whitetails, for passing whitetails definitely stop to check the odor left at these sites. Not only do rutting bucks frequently use this gland on overhead twigs, they flare it during displays of dominance, as do does when they are nursing their fawns.

• *Forehead glands* are thought to be used for scent marking. During autumn, whitetails of both sexes rub their foreheads on branches, depositing this gland's scent.

• *Interdigital glands* are found on all four feet in folds between the whitetail's toes. Although the purpose of this scent-making gland is unknown, it must, at the very least, serve as a means of leaving a scent trail. Such a trail would alert deer to the passing of one of their kind, an important message year-round, but especially during breeding season.

• Located about 6 inches above the hoof, the *metatarsal gland* is marked by a white tuft of hair on the outside of both rear legs. Interestingly, this gland is far larger in northern subspecies of whitetails. In black-tailed deer this gland has been proven to emit an odor that warns other deer of danger. Studies have failed to confirm that the whitetail uses this gland for the same purpose.

• The *tarsal gland* is large and significant, located on the inside of the whitetail's leg at the tarsal joint. It is marked by a raised tuft of long hairs. Like a large brush, this tuft becomes "painted" with the pheromones released from within, as well as with urine, which the deer deposits on this gland through a behavior called "rub urination" or "scent urination." In this technique deer of both sexes hunch up slightly and urinate on the inside of their rear legs. As the breeding season progresses, the tarsal gland of mature bucks becomes stained from the frequent rub urination, and the odor of it is detectable even by humans. The tarsal gland is generally considered by hunters to be the most important of the "communication" glands.

Glands secrete scents called pheromones that are important signals for other deer. The scent from each of these glands can send important messages, from the urgency to breed to the need to flee.

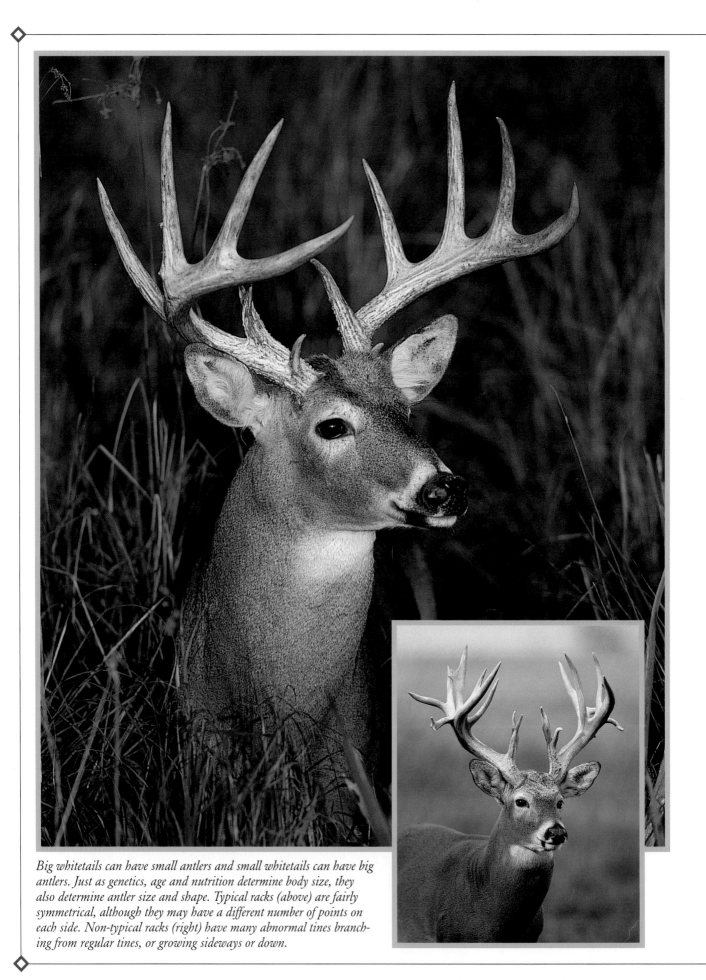

Big whitetails can have small antlers and small whitetails can have big antlers. Just as genetics, age and nutrition determine body size, they also determine antler size and shape. Typical racks (above) are fairly symmetrical, although they may have a different number of points on each side. Non-typical racks (right) have many abnormal tines branching from regular tines, or growing sideways or down.

Antler Growth and Purpose

Sure, antlers do serve the whitetail buck as weapons against predators and other whitetail rivals. But for the most part, these elaborate ornaments are there so bucks won't have to fight, at least among themselves. Social dominance in the male whitetail's world is largely governed by size of body and size of antlers. Since large bucks generally also produce large antlers, this headgear serves as a visual means of displaying one's status. Small bucks fear large bucks, limiting the rare actual combat to rivals of equal stature. Thus, in the grand evolutionary mastery of nature, these fascinating antlers, though they could be used for deadly means, prevent most fights simply through display.

Antlers are deciduous–grown and shed each year–and are actually made of bone and are living tissue. A cow's horns, on the other hand, are made of keratin, a dead tissue, and are not shed.

Bucks produce their first antlers in the spring just prior to their first

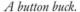

birthday, although fawn bucks sometimes grow short buttons (not to be confused with the longer "spikes" of some yearling bucks).

Antler growth is triggered by the pineal gland, which in turn triggers the release of testosterone, the hormone most responsible for antler growth. The pineal gland is sensitive to photoperiod; antler growth begins as the days lengthen in spring, between the spring equinox and summer solstice. Whitetails in the Far North have a more defined schedule to their antler growth than do those deer near the equator. For example, Minnesota bucks are growing antlers by May, while those in Florida don't start until June.

Antler growth is incredibly rapid, and is, in fact, the fastest growing bone known to science. Although antler growth is started by the lengthening of days in spring, it is hastened by the shortening days of late summer. By the time the rut occurs, antlers will have been hardened bone for two full months. Growing antlers are covered in a modified skin and fur known as velvet. Rich with blood and

A button buck.

During early growth, the velvet and the antler forming inside it are about 80 percent protein.

nerve tissues, velvet nourishes the growing bone, and consists almost completely of a protein called collagen. Antlers are susceptible to damage when in velvet, and an injured antler bleeds profusely, but clots quickly. Misshapen antlers are often a result of accidental damage during this growth period.

Antler velvet dies in early autumn and either falls off the hardened bone, or is scraped away on brush and trees by the buck. The color of the antler, which can range from near white to mahogany brown, is determined by the amount of blood staining during the velvet stripping process. Antlers are high in mineral content, which the buck will steal from his own skeleton if his diet provides inadequate amounts, replacing them from his diet once the antlers are fully hardened.

White-tailed deer antlers sweep forward on the main beam, then grow upward on the tines. This basket shape seems to be designed to "catch" the antlers of an equal-size opponent, thus lowering the risk of injury to either combatant.

Antler size is determined by both nutrition and genetics. That is, some deer just have the genes for big antlers, but even then, their antlers won't be as big as they could be without good nutrition. With both good nutrition and the right genes, a yearling buck (his second fall) may have three or four points per side. Lacking one or the other of these elements, his first rack may only consist of two single spikes.

Recent research also indicates that the doe, as well as the buck, contributes genes that control antler growth. Bucks continue to grow antlers all their lives, with their peak rack occurring when they are five-and-a-half years old. As they age beyond that, their antler size may diminish.

Antlers are cast in January through March, again as a reaction to photoperiod. At the point where the antler erupts from the skull is a joint known as the pedicle. Resulting from decreased testosterone after the rut, the bond between antler and pedicle weakens, and the two antlers fall off, often within hours of each other. In only a matter of a few short months, however, the buck will again start to grow antlers—the only regenerating living tissue in the animal world.

Usually both antlers do not drop off at the same time, but it is common to find both sheds within 100 yards of each other.

Most of the velvet is shed within 24 hours, but small pieces may remain on the antler for up to a week.

A LIFETIME OF ANTLERS

As a buck ages, it usually grows larger, thicker antlers. And throughout its life, consistent and unique antler characteristics make the deer easy to identify. This buck was photographed in November over the course of several years. As a 1½-year-old, the antlers are healthy. At 2½ years, the rack is showing its general shape. No photo was taken the next year, but as a 4½-year-old whitetail, the antlers are definitely gaining height. The fourth year photographed, the 5½-year-old deer now sports a massive rack with 10 points and a healthy, heavy body. The next year, at 6½ years, the deer's antler growth peaks with 17 points and an estimated score of 200 inches. The final year Bill Kinney was able to photograph this whitetail, it carries a nice 14-point rack and is 7½ years old.

1 ½ years old

2 ½ years old

4 1/2 years old

6 ½ years old

5 ½ years old

7 ½ years old

24

Breeding Behavior

It's the rule for all species: The greatest amount of each individual's effort goes into the breeding cycle or to the rearing of young. Life is no different for white-tailed deer–the effort to pass on its genes is the central mission in a deer's life. Everything a deer does–escaping predators, surviving winter, scent-marking trees, even just feeding–are simply steps toward successfully reproducing itself. Exactly how a deer goes about it, however, depends upon its sex.

Maturity and Success Rate

Even though some male whitetails reach puberty as fawns, and all are sexually mature as yearlings, they rarely breed. Breeding rights among bucks are determined by size, so they spend most of their early lives just trying to grow large and old enough to get a chance to breed. To this end, body size is more important than antler size. Forced to make a choice (physiologically, not consciously), a buck will divert scant nutritional resources to putting on size and weight, rather than antler growth, which consumes tremendous energy.

Once bucks mature at 3 to 5 years of age, they then exert enormous effort into ranging widely beyond their home range in an effort to find receptive mates. Since bucks spend years denied the chance to reproduce, once mature enough to outclass rivals, they reproduce with as many does as possible. This helps ensure some of their offspring will themselves live long enough to perpetuate their genetic contribution. This then could be called a buck's reproductive strategy: Grow big and range widely. A buck is the wind that scatters seed.

A doe's strategy is different. Her genetic contribution is carried, born and defended by her. She does not directly compete with other does for a mate. Although she grows restless during the breeding season and advertises her presence in her home range, she rarely needs to leave it to seek a mate, since he will invariably find her.

Thus, the doe's well-established home range may have a reproductive role–by staying in a small area, it is much easier for a mate to find you when you're ready to breed. If both sexes wandered widely during the breeding season, sexual encounters would be much more happenstance. Does, therefore, ensure their reproductive success by skillfully choosing habitat that provides the vast energy stores needed for a successful full-term pregnancy, offers a secure birthing area, is dense enough to hide fawns, and contains enough and appropriate food.

Among large mammals, white-tailed deer are considered a prolific species. They reach puberty at an early age (as fawns in some populations, as yearlings in all others). Exactly when they reach puberty has much to do with the quality of the range in which the deer is found, since the onset of puberty is determined by body weight. With good habitat and a population density within the carrying capacity of the habitat, fawns can reach the weight needed–70 pounds for southern deer, and 80 pounds for those in the North–by their first autumn.

In general, though, it is best for a population if fawns don't breed. Fawn does that do breed usually bear only one fawn, lack the birthing and rearing skills of older does, tend to breed later in the season (which results in later birthing dates that leave their fawns little time to grow before winter), and have a higher rate of stillbirths and fawn abandonment.

Fawn bucks (and yearlings) that breed in the absence of mature bucks have not been tested by the rigors of life. It is possible that these animals might never have attained the age or dominance status to breed, and so by mating early in life, possibly introduce inferior genetics to the population. Usually, nature ensures that this doesn't happen, but in populations where too many mature bucks have been removed, young bucks do get a chance to reproduce.

Most bucks don't reach their physical peak until they are 5 years old. In some heavily hunted areas, "old" bucks may merely be 3 1/2 years old; in more pristine settings, some bucks retain dominance status past 10 years of age.

Does are sexually active by the time they are yearlings. A doe's breeding success improves with age until she is about 8 years old. Once mature, she'll usually bear twins, and is a skillful mother. Given this scenario, a doe may have as many as eight or nine fawns before a same-age buck mates for the first time.

It's clear then that how quickly a deer population

Actual breeding activity begins with a courtship ritual, which is initiated when a buck catches a whiff of a doe in estrus.

grows depends upon the number of does. Think of the sex ratio in mathematical terms: does "multiply" while bucks "add or subtract." Does, of course, "multiply" themselves. Remove a doe from a population and you remove not just one deer, but at least two or three (the doe, and the one or two fawns she would have born the next spring), and perhaps even more if you consider that she might have lived to reproduce for a number of years. Remove a buck from the population and you merely subtract one deer.

Because of the early age at which does breed, and the number of fawns they can carry, white-tailed deer in good habitat can double their population in just two years, and even whitetail populations in poor habitat have the potential to grow by a factor of 1.7 in four years.

The Rut Begins

In autumn, as the days shorten, strange and wonderful things occur to bucks and does, building slowly at first, but eventually cresting in a wave of activity that is unmatched at any other time of the year. With the first cool September nights (in the North), whitetails' thoughts turn to reproduction. Both sexes begin to alter their behavior by changing their daily patterns and adding new, reproduction-centered behaviors. The rut is short and intense—so much so for the male of the species that he can destroy his own vitality, expending great energy in wandering and feeding so little that the effort can leave him vulnerable to the rigors of winter.

But the rut doesn't begin overnight. Gradually, as the days shorten, the old magic of photoperiod affects the pineal gland located deep in the brain, releasing the hormone melatonin. Now you may not care much about this chemical substance, but this hormone's influence starts the irreversible events that prepare each deer for reproduction.

For the does, the released melatonin is critical to the production of yet other hormones. New, elevated levels of the female hormone estrogen begin coursing through does causing physical changes, such as preparing her uterus to receive eggs. And while the picture of a swollen-necked, hormone-charged buck is familiar to us all, does also change behaviorally thanks to estrogen, gradually becoming more and more restless and increasing nighttime activity greatly as the rut peaks. Although she will usually stay within her home range, the doe's restless movements increase her odds of encountering a mate.

The same chemical melatonin that stirs the doe biologically and behaviorally triggers testosterone production in bucks. This primary male sex hormone first causes antlers to harden and velvet to shed, then drives him to battle with shrubs. Eventually, it forces him to sometimes battle other deer, to create buck scrapes and to wander widely. At the peak of the rut, bucks are sometimes so driven to distraction by this hormone, they often throw caution to the wind in their wandering. This inattention to their own welfare puts them at risk, making them more susceptible to both human and four-legged predators.

In the early phases of the rut period, bucks may thrash about in low-growing brush or shrubs. It is a good way to strengthen neck muscles for sparring with other bucks.

Antler Rubs and Dominance Hierarchies

In early September (in the North; later in the South), antlers harden and velvet is shed. As one would expect, these steps occur first in dominant bucks, since mature bucks produce more testosterone than their younger cohorts. As they are shedding their antler velvet, bucks begin to rub their antlers on brush and tree trunks. Although it was once thought that rubbing was done to remove velvet (which it may do to some small degree), it probably has other causes and purposes, since antler velvet sheds without this rubbing. The entire shedding process takes only about 24 hours. Given the amount of rubbing bucks are doing at this time, it is unlikely that it is governed simply by a desire to remove the velvet.

Instead, antler rubs probably signify the beginning of the dominance hierarchy among bucks. This rubbing may also help bucks determine the size and shape of their antlers. Mature bucks, because of their higher levels of testosterone, rub trees more frequently than young bucks and begin to do so much earlier in the autumn than subordinate bucks. The presence of a large number of antler rubs seen early in the autumn indicates that there's an old, dominant male in the vicinity. Dominant bucks also continue to rub trees well into, and sometimes even after, the rut. Yearling bucks make less than half as many antler rubs as dominant bucks, and begin to do so later in the fall (because they produce less testosterone).

Although bucks will rub just about anything with their antlers, including fence posts, they seem to prefer soft-barked trees. In some regions they seem to prefer trees that produce pungent sap, such as balsam fir, spruce, cedar or hemlock, perhaps because these trees enhance scent-marking. Remember that whitetails have a forehead gland, so that beyond just testing their antlers, bucks are leaving a chemical marker for their rivals and potential mates. Antler rubs, particularly those made during the actual rut, are often along buck "highways," routes used for many years.

It is commonly believed by hunters, although not confirmed by science, that big bucks rub larger trees. Since it is well known that some large trees are used year after year for this ritual, and that large dominant bucks do most of the antler rubbing, the "big tree—big buck" hypothesis is probably at least partially true.

During the pre-rut stage, bucks are doing things other than thrashing trees. They are finalizing the "pecking order" that they had been working on all summer in their bachelor groups. As the levels of testosterone rise, bucks begin to test each other in sparring matches. These aren't the all-out battles that sometimes occur in the rut. Bucks test each other more gently, locking antlers carefully so that they don't injure each other. These brief tests, most often initiated by the younger bucks, are tolerated by the dominant animal. These sparring matches allow deer to "size each other up," crystallizing the dominance hierarchy. Later, during the rut when the bucks will be stressed enough just by their extensive travels, this pecking order will eliminate many fights, saving needed energy, leaving the true battles for bucks that encounter an equal-size rival.

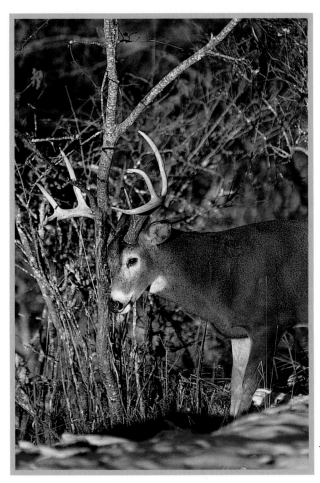

A typical rub tree has smooth bark, few lower branches and is about 1 inch in diameter. But rub trees can vary in size from ½ to 4 inches.

ILLINOIS PRAIRIE DISTRICT LIBRARY

Doe Behavior

While much attention in research and literature is generally afforded bucks during this period, does are no less affected. As the rut intensifies she goes through some conflicting urges. She becomes less protective of this year's fawns, and so will allow her yearlings of the previous year to rejoin her, forming larger, family units. However, does will not allow the return of their yearling buck offspring, who probably just got kicked out of the bachelor group as testosterone levels made everyone a bit testy. If he returns to his mother, she will drive him mercilessly away, to avoid his breeding with her or any other of his near relatives. Even a mother's tolerance of yearling and fawn daughters isn't unconditional. Once she enters her estrous cycle and impatiently awaits her mate, she seeks solitude. Her daughters will only be allowed to rejoin her after she's mated.

As she succumbs to the inevitable urges of hormones, a doe becomes increasingly restless, often at night. Within her home range is a section that she considers her "core" area. Like the buck that wanders and advertises his presence through rubs and scrapes, the intense use of this core area causes her scent to permeate the vicinity, helping to attract bucks to her home.

A doe's urine provides the most important clues to wandering bucks about her condition to breed. About 20 days before she enters "heat" or estrus, rising levels of progesterone are revealed in her urine. This serves as a chemical odor clue detectable by any passing buck. Does sometimes pause to urinate when they know a buck is following them. If she isn't ready to mate, she saves herself the trouble of avoiding his sexual overtures, which also saves the buck the energy he might otherwise expend in the chase.

Actual estrus lasts between 24 and 48 hours. Mature does in good physical condition enter estrus before young does, or does that are in poor shape. Fawn does that do experience estrus do so late in the breeding season, sometimes into December and January, even in the North. If a doe isn't bred during her first estrous cycle, she'll enter a second estrous cycle in about a month.

Buck Behavior

In the full grip of hormonal overload, bucks seek mates by extending their travels. Home ranges increase in size up to 3 square miles, and truly superb dominant bucks, called "dominant floaters" by biologists, roam over a large territory. These bucks fear few rivals, and enter the home range of other, but smaller, dominant bucks, usurping the breeding rights as they pass through. Sometimes called "hermit" bucks by hunters, these superb specimens are usually at least 5½ years old.

White-tailed bucks aren't truly territorial. They will tolerate the presence of other breeding-age bucks as long as these other bucks exhibit subordinate behavior. There is some evidence that does seek to breed with the most genetically superior buck available. When unable to drive a young suitor away, does have been known to lead him to a big buck that will finish the job of driving him off. In such cases, the subordinate buck literally high-tails it out of the vicinity without risking a confrontation. True dominance battles generally only take place between equal rivals.

Dominance fights rarely lead to death, but that outcome does occur. Sometimes the combatants' antlers become locked, leading to the death of one or both. Bucks have been seen with the entire

Both bucks and does visit and urinate in scrapes to leave messages. Bucks urinate over their tarsal gland, while does urinate directly into the scrape.

Sparring and fighting between bucks of similar size is one way to set the dominance hierarchy of breeding rights.

head and rack of a rival still locked in theirs, apparently able to paw themselves free of the rival's dead body with their sharp hooves. Injuries, such as puncture wounds or eye loss, also occur. Yet both death and injury are fairly rare. The whitetail's rack, with its basket shape, is designed to "catch" an opponent, not spear him, lowering the risk of serious injury or death. In addition, most dominance fights are short lived—less than a minute. It is better for the "loser" to break off the fight and flee so that he might breed elsewhere than to risk death or injury battling a superior rival.

Buck Scrapes

Testosterone levels continue to increase in northern bucks into October, peaking near the middle of the month. It is no coincidence that this is also when bucks begin to make ground scrapes. Bucks in the Southeast start making scrapes in November, while those in the Southwest take on this task in December.

Buck scrapes are an important form of whitetail communication. They let other bucks know who's boss of the neighborhood, and they also serve to let does know that a breeding-age buck will again be passing this way. Scrapes are a message, a note made of odors, and the dominant buck's way of asserting himself even when he can't physically be present.

Although bucks are still making antler rubs at this time, these sign posts begin to play a subordinate role as the rut intensifies. Scrapes become the most important message-bearing device, and unlike antler rubs, which are often made in dense cover, scrapes frequently are made where the understory is more open. Bucks choose these sites to maximize their "advertising" potential—they are usually on or along well-worn trails, and are frequently found on high ground (which may help make their

SCRAPING AND RUBBING ACTIVITY BY AGE CLASS OF BUCKS

Research conducted in Michigan's upper peninsula (Ozoga and Verme) found that 3- to 8-year-old bucks begin scraping and rubbing earlier than 1½-year-old bucks.

For both groups, scraping reached its maximum level during November 3 to 9, about 14 days before the peak week of breeding—November 17 to 23.

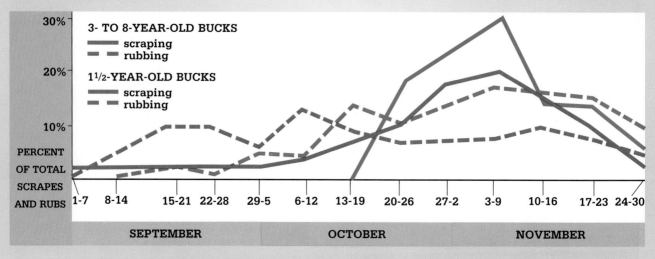

scent carry farther). They are also often clustered near each other.

One well-worn buck route where I hunt has scrapes every 40 to 50 yards for a length of ¼ mile, after which they become much less frequent. It may be just coincidence, but this cluster is also in an area heavily used for bedding sites by a group of does. The message seems to be "I'm around, and I'll be back."

Usually these scrapes are 3 or 4 feet across, although they can be much larger. Almost invariably there will be an overhead branch, some 3 to 5 feet above the scrape site, frequently with a bare, broken tip. The buck licks this branch tip, and rubs his forehead and orbital (eye socket) gland on it. It is also possible that he deposits scent from his nasal glands. Licking of the limb tip may transfer other scent-producing materials, such as residue from the tarsal gland, which he sometimes pauses to lick. After completing this task, he scrapes the earth bare of leaves and grass with his front hooves. While pawing, he probably deposits some scent from the interdigital glands, which are found between his toes.

The real scent-marking, however, occurs when the buck rub-urinates into the middle of the scrape. Hunching slightly, the buck urinates down the inside of his rear legs while rubbing his tarsal glands together. This scent-marking routine continues through the rut, peaking about two weeks before the majority of does enter estrus.

About half of the scrape sites will be re-worked by their maker, often intensely over a short period. He may just as mysteriously ignore them for days or weeks, then begin using them again. Once the rut is in full swing, dominant bucks usually cease to freshen their scrapes, probably because they've got more work than they can handle by mating with willing does. At this point, a buck no longer needs to advertise his presence to them.

Does, on the other hand, sometimes leave scent messages of their own by urinating near these scrapes. The scent messages they receive from buck scrapes may even be important to stimulating their own estrous cycle, and the scents they leave probably help the scrape-maker determine where does are located, and their readiness to breed.

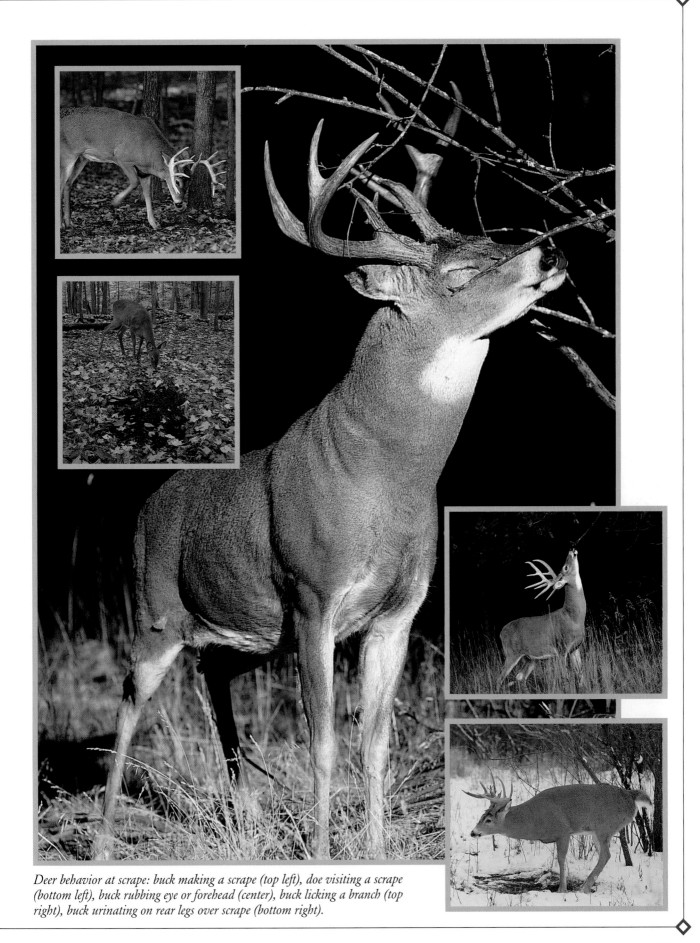

Deer behavior at scrape: buck making a scrape (top left), doe visiting a scrape (bottom left), buck rubbing eye or forehead (center), buck licking a branch (top right), buck urinating on rear legs over scrape (bottom right).

The Mating Game

While all this scent-marking and sign-posting is going on, deer are evaluating each other as mates or rivals. By the time the rut is fully engaged, and the does start coming into estrus, bucks have nearly worn themselves out traveling over a large area, in some cases, thousands of acres. By early November in the North, and a month or two later in the South, the prime-age, prime-condition does will be in estrus and cease running away from bucks. Up until the estrous cycle came into full swing, dominant bucks traveled largely at night, so a sure sign that the rut is peaking is the sight of mature bucks during the daylight hours. Before it's all over, dominant bucks may lose 20 percent or more of their body weight in their around-the-clock, never-ending pursuit.

When a buck pursues her, a doe in estrus often pauses to urinate. When bucks encounter the urine, they stop to lick it and then perform what is called the lip-curling flehmen. Not only does this act tell him if the doe is ready to mate, it may be important to prepare himself for copulation. If he is convinced she is ready, he follows her rather politely in short, choppy steps, holding his head low and neck outstretched. When doing this, or trailing her, a buck might emit short, low noises called a "tending grunt." But just because she allows him to tend her, it doesn't mean she's fully ready to mate. Until she is ready to allow actual physical contact, she may lead the buck in circles for as much as a day, during which he "courts" her patiently.

After they mate, the pair may separate, or may stay together for up to another full day. If they do remain together, some pairs mate a second time. Once they separate, the doe returns to her normal routine while the buck continues to pursue his amorous ways. Because does expend less energy than bucks during the rut, they enter winter in

To perform the lip curl, the buck extends his neck, holds his snout slightly upward and curls back his upper lip to close the nasal chamber, which intensifies the urine odor, helping to determine the doe's stage of estrus.

much better physical condition. Although we tend to think of big bucks as the very finest physical specimens, they expend so much energy during the rut that they are second only to fawns in winter mortality.

Eventually, the rut ceases. But like its beginning, it doesn't happen abruptly. Decreasing daylight again causes photoreceptive responses in both bucks and does, slowing the mating urge. Those does not bred during the first cycle will come into estrus about a month later. Bucks with enough testosterone still coursing through their veins will find and mate with them. But gradually, and surely, the rush to reproduce ends. Deer travel to winter habitats to pass the winter. Does concentrate on preserving their strength so that it might go to nourish the embryos they carry. Bucks seek a rest to regain their lost vigor, and by January or February, will drop the impressive racks that they had grown at such an expense.

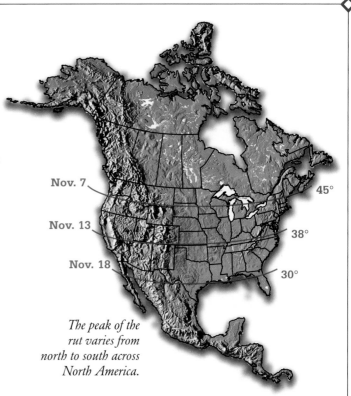

Nov. 7

Nov. 13

Nov. 18

45°

38°

30°

The peak of the rut varies from north to south across North America.

A buck may continue tending a doe for several more days after they breed, defending her from other bucks.

Home ranges vary in size and shape according to the terrain and perhaps deer density in the area. Ranges of mature bucks (red circle) often overlap many doe ranges (white circles).

Habitats and Home Ranges

For most of its life, the average white-tailed deer lives in an area of about 1 square mile, often called its "home range," where it finds its basic needs—security cover, food and water. In the North where special winter cover is necessary for survival, whitetails may have a second, separate "winter range," or deer yard. This may be located adjacent to, or even in, its regular home range, or it may be many miles away.

Most home ranges are oval. Fidelity to home ranges is strong. Deer have starved to death in their home range, even though better browse existed within just a few miles. That bond may be so strong because it is generally learned while a deer follows its mother through her daily and seasonal routine. Because does pass on this knowledge to their own offspring, which will then pass it on to

their own young, generations of related deer often utilize the same home range.

Bucks seem to have a larger home range than do does, and are particularly prone to wandering during the breeding season. Don't think of a home range as a place that encompasses all the deer in that vicinity. Home ranges are unique to the individual, and while a doe and her fawns may have exactly the same range until the fawns mature (and even afterward, if they are females), bucks and other doe-groups in that area will probably have a different range. These ranges do overlap, however, putting the deer in contact with each other.

Bucks select a slightly different range than does based on their antler-growth nutritional demands. Does select a home range that favors the rearing of young. The ranges of the two sexes overlap least during the fawning season and most during the winter.

HOME RANGE SIZE BY ACRES

Buck and doe home ranges vary in size throughout the year. Data from 20 years of radio-tracking in Texas show that adult bucks during fall have the largest home ranges. This is the result of mature bucks traveling through several doe home ranges searching for a doe in estrus.

	Buck Fawns	Yearling Bucks	Adult Bucks	Doe Fawns	Yearling Does	Adult does
SPRING	310	450	410	390	210	190
SUMMER	160	410	350	160	105	145
FALL	140	675	1090	110	260	275
WINTER	150	310	290	275	300	400

Winter Changes

Whitetails in the North shift from their home range to their winter range in response to sharp drops in temperature. This is important to hunters, because this shift can occur during hunting season. If you've scouted your chosen hunting grounds in early fall, and your hunt occurs after the first snowfall or prolonged cold snap, you may find that the deer are no longer using the same trails, bedding areas or feeding grounds that you discovered in September. It pays, then, to learn just what winter habitat looks like, so that you'll be able to adjust.

Winter deer yards are most often located in areas of dense conifers. A conifer's dense foliage and conical shape help to deflect snow away from the ground beneath, leaving areas of less snow where deer can move more freely. In addition, whitetails create networks of trails through the yards to further enhance movement. Because conifers are dark in color, they also serve as solar collectors, creating a warmer micro-climate beneath them. By bedding beneath such thick overhead cover, which reduces heat loss to the sky, a deer's body heat loss is further minimized. Winter cover is crucial to whitetail survival in the North. Those deer with access to such deer yards frequently survive conditions that kill other deer whose range lacks adequate stands of conifers.

Even winter cover can be segregated into two types: bedding and browsing. The best bedding areas are about 80 percent conifer, while the browsing areas will be comprised of about 60 percent conifer—enough conifers to keep the snow depth down, but with adequate space in the canopy through which sunlight can pass so that woody browse can grow. Upland cedar probably provides the best winter cover since not only does it deflect snow and retain thermal energy, it is also a very nutritious browse. Hemlock is also a good choice, followed by lowland cedar groves. Balsam fir and spruce groves are a bit further down the list—they provide good winter cover but are poor dietary fare. Still further down the list are the pines: jack, white and Norway. Because they have more open crowns than other conifers, pines aren't as efficient at intercepting snow, and none have much food value.

Southern whitetails generally travel less than northern deer because they don't face such severe winter challenges. That doesn't mean they don't migrate. Some movement occurs to take advantage of seasonal food sources or to avoid flooding. Generally, though, the greater the extremes in weather, the farther a deer will move in both the span of a year and over its lifetime. It is believed that in those populations of whitetails that must migrate long distances to winter habitat, fawns learn the complex route from their mothers. Some researchers believe that the deer in a particular winter yard are all closely related and come from the same, or adjacent, summer ranges. Thus, if a massive die-off in that deer yard occurs, the summer range that would have been utilized by those deer will largely remain vacant.

Deep snow can trap deer in areas with limited food supply. If the snow persists, some deer may starve. If necessary, deer can fast for several weeks in winter, so only extended cold and deep snow pose a serious problem.

Geographical Variations

Whitetails are amazingly adaptable animals. They are found in nearly every state and province, from sub-tropical Florida to the Northern Great Plains. This means that the types of habitat they can inhabit varies greatly by region.

A hunter in the Great Lakes states, for instance, will likely seek out mixed deciduous forests. In the more northerly part of this range, young aspen forests will provide both good whitetail habitat, and hunting opportunities. In the southern part of this range, and throughout the mid-latitude states, forest with adjacent acorn crops can support very large populations of whitetails.

On the Central and Northern Plains, whitetails most often are found along river bottoms and in the occasional woodlot, from which they can venture out to feed on farm crops. Wetland areas, with dense stands of cattails, are particularly good hiding cover for whitetails, and can be a real challenge to hunt. Similarly, standing corn can hide an entire herd of whitetails, and, provided you have the landowner's permission, is a great place to practice your stalking skills.

In drier regions of the Plains and Mountain states, water becomes a critical factor both for whitetails and those who pursue them. Typically, foothills of the dry mountains will have the most consistent watering areas, whether they take the form of ponds or creeks. Stock ponds, created by farmers and ranchers, serve a similar purpose. Hunting near natural or artificial watering areas is a sound strategy in these parts of the country.

No matter where you hunt, keep your eyes peeled for three types of habitat: bedding/hiding areas, which are typically dense, and often elevated so that the deer can see; travel corridors, through which deer move from resting places to feeding grounds; and feeding areas. Travel corridors are most often located in low areas, where deer can pass without being seen. Creek bottoms and draws are good places to look.

Feeding areas are often either the easiest or most

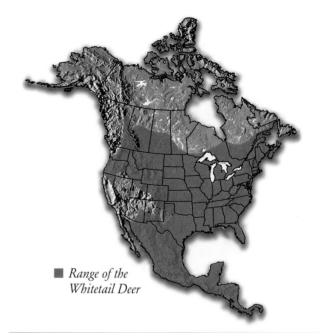

■ *Range of the*
Whitetail Deer

Southern (left), Mountain (below) and Midwest (bottom) regions all support deer populations, each offering a variety of habitat advantages and disadvantages.

Texas and the Southwest (top) offer deer lots of wide-open spaces, while deer living in the North or Great Lakes areas (above) often have deep cover for protection.

difficult to find. In places with truly defined food sources, such as crop fields or stands of oak trees, it is quickly obvious where deer are feeding. But in many places, whitetails feed on a variety of plants, and so can essentially make a living just about anywhere. In these places, patterning deer is much more difficult, and hunters would be wise to instead focus on hunting near naturally defined corridors.

During most of the year, and throughout much of their geographic range, white-tailed deer can choose from a variety of succulent plants. Their diet changes with the seasons and with their physiological requirements, and those needs are different for deer of different ages or sex.

For instance, does are severely stressed just before they wean their nursing fawns in early autumn, but bucks are at their nutritional peak, having spent the summer building reserves for what is their biggest challenge—the rut. Mature bucks weigh 30 percent more than same-age females, but have a lower metabolic rate. This seems to allow them to subsist on poorer fare than can does; the does' dependency on more nutritious foods is likely related to the energy requirements of pregnancy and nursing.

Whitetails in the Southwest frequently consume prickly pear cactus during the summer, while their cousins in the Southeast are eating grapes, and midwestern whitetails are eating late varieties of berries. Fruits (often referred to as soft mast) are, by the way, a much favored food of whitetails wherever they live. The variety they eat is only limited by the location and season—apples, blueberries, persimmons, blackberries and huckleberries are among the most desirable. Obviously, whitetails in more southerly latitudes enjoy an advantage in this regard, since warmer weather and longer growing seasons provide more of a bounty.

But it is the succulent parts of woody plants that are the most important component of the whitetail's diet. Leafy portions of trees and shrubs, such as red-osier dogwood, aspen, oak and an array of vines, find their way frequently to the whitetail's menu.

When plentiful, especially in fall and winter, acorns can make up as much as 60 percent of a deer's diet.

Food Sources

In some areas, agricultural plants are an important source of nutrition, and deer eat not only the ripened plant, but the seeds and fresh shoots as well. Woodland-bound whitetails without access to farm crops do fine by substituting leaf-bearing annuals and perennials from the forest floor, such as aster and clover. Even plants we consider toxic, like poison ivy and inedible mushrooms, are digestible for the adaptable whitetail.

Mast, such as acorns, is an important food in season, particularly autumn. Whitetails also eat both red and white cedar. The white cedar is considered the only woody browse capable of sustaining whitetails through the winter and is a critical food source in the North. Unlike whitetails in the South, those in the most northerly range are often forced in winter to subsist on less-desirable forage such as woody browse, the least digestible.

The home range of a deer isn't large. But the deer knows it as well as you know the inside of your home. There are no shortcuts to becoming a master of whitetail hunting. You must learn at least the basics of whitetail feeding, mating and travel strategies before you'll truly stand a chance of catching one off guard.

Diseases

Whitetails are robust animals, and generally aren't susceptible to a lot of health problems. However, in recent decades, some "new" diseases have sprung up that not only impact some white-tailed deer, but may also be transmitted to humans. Hunters, because of their contact with deer during field dressing and butchering, are at a higher risk than the general public.

Lyme Disease

Lyme disease was named in 1977 when arthritis was observed in a cluster of children in and around Lyme, Connecticut. The disease is still largely a problem in the Northeast and Great Lakes region. Not truly a disease of the whitetail, since they serve primarily as a host of the tick (below) that transmits the disease, it is included here because these ticks are common on deer, and may transfer to a hunter.

The deer tick (*Ixodes dammini*) is responsible for most of the cases of Lyme disease in the United States. The tick has three life stages: larva, nymph and adult. Each stage takes a single blood meal. The bite is painless so most victims do not know they have been bitten. The nymphal stage appears to be responsible for most Lyme disease cases. The adult ticks (about the size of a sesame seed) prefer to feed on white-tailed deer. The entire life cycle requires three separate hosts and takes about two years to complete.

About half of the humans who've contracted Lyme disease develop a characteristic rash a few days to a few weeks after the bite from an infected tick. The rash generally looks like an expanding red ring. At about the same time that the rash develops, flu-like symptoms may appear with headache, sore throat, stiff neck, fever, muscle aches, fatigue and general malaise. Some people develop the flu-like illness without getting a rash. Hunters should check themselves thoroughly after handling a deer to ensure they've not become a host to a deer tick.

Bovine Tuberculosis

Bovine tuberculosis (TB) is a contagious respiratory disease caused by the bacterium Mycobacterium bovis, and can infect most warm-blooded animals, including humans. The federal government has done nationwide testing of cattle herds to control bovine TB, but it still occurs in cattle, penned exotic livestock such as elk, and wild deer. TB has been diagnosed in captive elk herds in several states. Michigan has found TB in its free-ranging white-tailed deer since 1994.

Although it rarely occurs, bovine TB can be transmitted to people. TB is generally transmitted through the air by coughing and sneezing, and it is highly unlikely a person would contract the disease from field dressing or eating the meat of an infected deer. However, it is always a good idea to wear gloves when field dressing any animal. There is no specific test that can be easily done to check for TB in deer meat. Michigan recommends any deer meat collected from a TB infected area not be smoked or made into sausage or jerky, but be thoroughly cooked until it is no longer pink, and juice from the meat runs clear.

Chronic Wasting Disease

Chronic wasting disease (CWD) occurs in North American deer and elk. It belongs to a group of infectious diseases known as "transmissible spongiform encephalopathies" (TSEs), the most famous of which is the well-known mad cow disease. It is caused by an abnormal protein called a prion which affects the animal's brain and is invariably fatal. Usually, months to years pass from the time an animal is infected to when it shows signs of the disease.

Whitetails that have contracted the disease sometimes display visible signs, such as drooping head or ears, poor body condition, tremors, stumbling, increased salivation, difficulty swallowing, or excessive thirst or urination. The disease was first discovered in Colorado and Wyoming, and at the time of this writing, has been discovered in wild or captive deer or elk in South Dakota, Nebraska, Kansas, Oklahoma, New Mexico, Montana, Minnesota, Wisconsin, Illinois, Saskatchewan and Alberta. Several wildlife agencies have decided to reduce the density of animals in the infected area to slow the transmission of the disease. In Colorado, Nebraska and Wisconsin, large numbers of animals are being killed to accomplish this.

To date, there is no known case of CWD infecting a human, although the risk remains. The closely related mad cow disease has been known to jump the species barrier to people, which has resulted in a number of human deaths.

Hunters can minimize their exposure and risk by following several precautions. Don't eat meat from animals that look sick or ill, and don't touch or eat the brain, spinal cord, eyes, spleen, tonsils or lymph nodes. In fact, it is important that you not cut into or through these body parts while field dressing or butchering. Prions can be spread, and they cannot be killed by cooking. In fact, they are virtually indestructible. The best defense is to not spread them from the above body parts, where they are known to be found.

Although the origin of CWD remains clouded, it has become clear that the movement of the disease from state to state is the result of the transfer of infected game-farm elk and deer. Inevitably, some of these animals either escape or come in contact with wild deer, and the dangerous release of this disease into a new region is complete.

Just about every state wildlife agency has increased its efforts to watch for CWD. To slow the spread of this disease, many states have now banned the importation of deer and elk. These game-farm animals are known to be a primary cause of CWD moving so rapidly around the U.S. and Canada. Some states have also banned supplemental feeding programs and the baiting of deer, because close contact between deer facilitates the spread of the disease. Hunters who travel should study regulations carefully because several states have implemented regulations that allow only boned meat, quarters (without spinal column or head) or processed meat from deer or elk to be transported out of certain areas with CWD. Other states have limited the importation of hunter-killed deer and elk to only boned or processed meat.

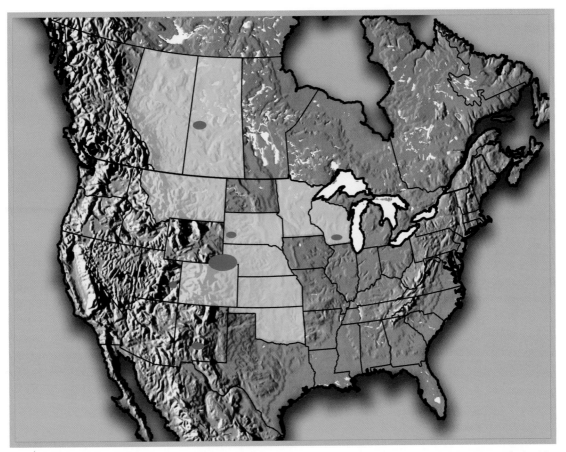

States and provinces in North America where CWD was found in captive animal populations are marked with yellow. Areas with CWD-infected wild populations are marked in red.

CHAPTER TWO

Equipment for Whitetail Hunting

Depending on where and when you hunt for whitetails, you may choose different equipment for different occasions.

The right rifle, for instance, makes your hunt more enjoyable and boosts your odds for success. Shotguns are widely used for deer hunting in agricultural or densely populated areas where rifle hunting is not allowed. Some southern states also permit the use of shotguns with buckshot.

With a muzzleloader, you'd better make your first shot count because it'll likely be your only shot. Many states have muzzleloader-only seasons, allowing you to extend your time afield and escape the hunting pressure of regular firearms seasons. Using handguns also increases the challenge of hunting whitetails. They do, additionally, allow some disabled hunters to enjoy the sport.

Bowhunting for whitetails was once enjoyed by only a few highly skilled archers. But new designs have made the bow easier to shoot accurately and opened the door to many more hunters.

Clothes for deer hunting should keep you quiet, safe and comfortable. A good tip when choosing accessories is to travel light with a pack containing only what you need–don't overload yourself with gadgets.

Rifles and Ammunition

A wide range of rifles and calibers are suitable for deer hunting. Selecting the right rifle for your needs is a personal decision that should be based on thoughtful consideration of action, caliber, fit and sights.

Actions

A rifle action is the mechanical means used to deliver a cartridge from the magazine to the chamber. The simplest action is the single shot, where the shooter places the cartridge in the chamber. The single shot is preferred by some marksmen who enjoy shooting these lightweight, accurate and reliable rifles.

Consistent accuracy and reliability make bolt actions the most popular rifles. Bolt-action rifles are available from most manufacturers in a wide selection of calibers. Scopes are easily mounted on them.

The lever-action rifle, recognizable from countless western movies, is a traditional deer-hunting favorite. Although they've been eclipsed in popularity by bolt actions, levers are still chosen by hunters who prefer a quick, lightweight gun.

Popular rifle actions include (left to right): falling block, lever action, bolt action, pump or "slide" action, semi-automatic or "autoloader." Each offers advantages for different hunting situations.

Knowing the parts of your rifle (right) will help you learn how it works, making you a better shot. Ballistics tables can help you determine the best caliber and cartridge for your type of hunting (opposite page).

Horizontal Adjustment

Vertical Adjustment

Scope Ring

Variable-power Ring

Scope

Scope Mount

Bolt Handle

Safety

Recoil Pad

Stock

Magazine

Trigger

Magazine Release

Trigger Guard

Sling

Sling Swivel

Pump actions are worked by moving the forearm, a physical action that comes naturally to many shooters, especially those who use pump-action shotguns for bird hunting. Pumps can be fired rapidly, but may jam in hunting situations.

Semi-automatic actions are worked by the expanding gases of a fired round. Although they can be shot as quickly as you can pull the trigger, semi-autos are prone to failure if they become dirty in cold or wet weather.

Calibers

Advances in cartridges and bullet performance give today's deer hunter an unprecedented selection of loads to choose from. The caliber you select should be appropriate for you and your hunting situation.

Whitetails have relatively thin skin and light bone structure. With proper shot placement, they can be killed by bullets delivering at least

900 foot-pounds of energy at the point of impact. This rules out the small-caliber cartridges, such as .22s. Most states and provinces have minimum caliber standards.

Although they have fallen out of favor with some modern hunters, low-velocity, medium-caliber cartridges such as the 30.30 Winchester, .300 Savage and .35 Remington were long the standard rounds for deer hunters, especially east of the Mississippi. The famous Model 94 Winchester lever action, typically chambered for .30-30, is by far the all-time best-selling American hunting rifle. The limitation of low-velocity cartridges is that they are restricted to ranges of 150 yards or less, which usually isn't a problem in the whitetail woods. The advantage is these calibers are often found in light, easy-to-carry guns. Bullet weights of 150 to 170 grains are recommended. For lever actions with tubular magazines, be sure to use round-nose bullets, because a pointed bullet could fire a round in the magazine from recoil.

Barrel

Fore-end

High-velocity, smaller calibers, such as the 6mm Remington, .243 Winchester, 25.06 Remington, .257 Roberts, .260 Remington and 7mm-08 are effective to 250 yards or more and capable of tack-driving accuracy. The disadvantage is the calibers have smaller bullets. Most hunters who use these calibers prefer bullets weighing at least 100 grains. Mild recoil and light-weight guns are advantages to these calibers, especially for children or women.

High-velocity, medium calibers offer the most versatility in loads and typically have adequate downrange energy to 300 yards or more. Popular calibers include the .270 Winchester, .280 Remington, 7mm Remington, 30.06 Springfield and .308 Winchester. Bullet weights may range from 130 to 220 grains, with 150 to 180 grains being the most common. These calibers are also suitable for larger game, such as elk and caribou.

Relatively new additions to deer hunting calibers are the short magnums, which achieve magnum performance with shorter cases and have noticeably less recoil. Short magnums come in .243, .270, 7mm and .300 calibers. They are well suited to long-range shooting, having flat trajectory and retaining energy at distances exceeding 300 yards.

Magnum calibers are better suited to larger game such as elk and moose, but are also used by some deer hunters. Calibers such as the .300 Winchester Magnum and .338 Winchester Magnum are best suited to long-range shooting or hunting especially large, northern white-tailed bucks. These are not calibers for beginners and they have substantial recoil many shooters find uncomfortable. The recoil can be tamed

BALLISTICS TABLE FOR COMMON CALIBERS

The first number is energy (in foot-pounds) and the second is trajectory (in inches above (+) or below (−) line of aim).

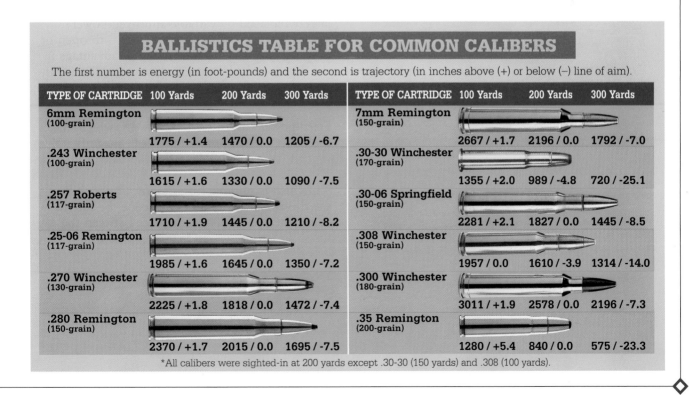

TYPE OF CARTRIDGE	100 Yards	200 Yards	300 Yards
6mm Remington (100-grain)	1775 / +1.4	1470 / 0.0	1205 / -6.7
.243 Winchester (100-grain)	1615 / +1.6	1330 / 0.0	1090 / -7.5
.257 Roberts (117-grain)	1710 / +1.9	1445 / 0.0	1210 / -8.2
.25-06 Remington (117-grain)	1985 / +1.6	1645 / 0.0	1350 / -7.2
.270 Winchester (130-grain)	2225 / +1.8	1818 / 0.0	1472 / -7.4
.280 Remington (150-grain)	2370 / +1.7	2015 / 0.0	1695 / -7.5

TYPE OF CARTRIDGE	100 Yards	200 Yards	300 Yards
7mm Remington (150-grain)	2667 / +1.7	2196 / 0.0	1792 / -7.0
.30-30 Winchester (170-grain)	1355 / +2.0	989 / -4.8	720 / -25.1
.30-06 Springfield (150-grain)	2281 / +2.1	1827 / 0.0	1445 / -8.5
.308 Winchester (150-grain)	1957 / 0.0	1610 / -3.9	1314 / -14.0
.300 Winchester (180-grain)	3011 / +1.9	2578 / 0.0	2196 / -7.3
.35 Remington (200-grain)	1280 / +5.4	840 / 0.0	575 / -23.3

*All calibers were sighted-in at 200 yards except .30-30 (150 yards) and .308 (100 yards).

POPULAR RIFLE SIGHTS

Even the best rifle is of little use without an accurate sighting device. Some hunters spend as much for a telescopic sight as for the rifle itself.

Open sights have a front post, which must be centered in the notched rear sight. They are the most difficult type to align because part of the target becomes covered.

Peep sights require you to center the target in a hole in the rear sight, then place the front bead on the animal. Large peepholes are easiest to use.

Scopes like this 4-Plex reticle, with their easy-to-use crosshairs, are the most popular. You can aim precisely, without obscuring the animal.

with a muzzle brake system, but at the expense of a much louder report that can damage your hearing.

When shooting short magnum or magnum loads for deer, bullet selection is especially important. Be sure to choose a bullet designed to kill deer at the ranges you are likely to shoot. At short ranges, be especially careful with shot placement to minimize damage to meat.

Fit

Most deer hunting rifles weigh between 6 and 9 pounds. Increasingly, hunters are choosing bolt-action rifles weighing less than 7 pounds without a scope, although recoil may be excessive in larger calibers. When buying a rifle, go to a gun shop and try several makes and styles. The gun should come easily to your shoulder when wearing hunting clothing. Work the action and the safety to determine the style you prefer.

Rifles come with wooden stocks and blued actions and barrels, or with all-weather synthetic stocks and stainless-steel barrels. The type you select is a matter of personal preference. Most rifles sold today have a recoil pad suitable for the caliber. On older, used guns, you may need to have a recoil pad installed by a gunsmith. Trigger pull, which should be adjusted by a gunsmith, is typically set at about 3.5 pounds.

Sights

With the exception of many lever-action and single-shot guns, open and peep sights have been largely replaced by variable and fixed-power scopes. Shooters who are proficient with open or peep sights are by no means at a disadvantage in the deer woods. However, scopes offer the advantage of magnification and improved light-gathering capabilities in low-light situations.

Fixed-power scopes are typically 4X, which makes the target easier to see, but doesn't magnify it so much that it is difficult to find and aim at a moving deer. Variable scopes range from 1.5X up to 9X, which is suitable for virtually all deer hunting situations. When mounting a scope, be sure to adjust the eye relief—the distance between the scope and your eye—so that you have a full field of vision. The scope should be far enough from your eye so it doesn't strike you from recoil.

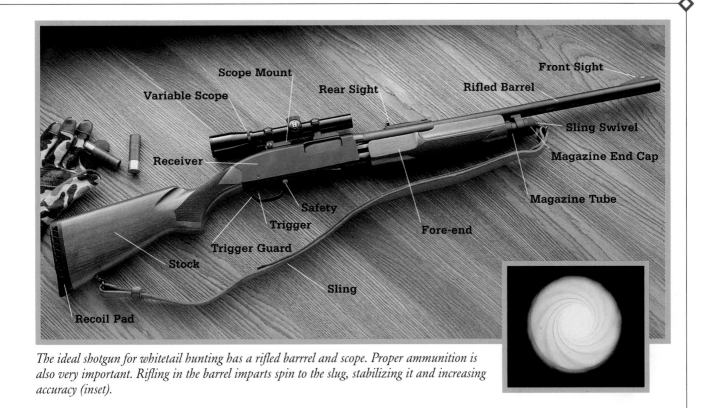

The ideal shotgun for whitetail hunting has a rifled barrrel and scope. Proper ammunition is also very important. Rifling in the barrel imparts spin to the slug, stabilizing it and increasing accuracy (inset).

Shotguns and Ammunition

In farm country or more densely populated areas, hunters are usually prohibited from using rifles because of the long distance a bullet may travel, posing a safety risk.

In these areas, shotguns are the preferred alternative. A properly configured shotgun can be a very effective short-range (100 yards) whitetail firearm. A 12-gauge shotgun is the best choice, and a 20-gauge is the absolute minimum a hunter should consider.

Chokes

The constriction at the muzzle end of a shotgun barrel—the choke—is there to increase muzzle velocity and tighten the shot string by compressing both the shotgun pellets and the gas propelling it. However, a choke that does a good job on bird loads may be too tight for slugs, causing erratic accuracy by deforming the projectile. Although almost any shotgun with an open choke can be used to hunt whitetails, the best

shotgun for deer hunting will have a rifled barrel and some type of additional sights. In some cases, you can buy an extra barrel for your favorite pump or semi-automatic bird gun, allowing it to perform double-duty. If a rifled barrel is not available for your gun, consider buying a barrel that has an open choke—improved cylinder or skeet.

Barrels and Scopes

A rifled barrel will allow a shotgun to shoot slugs accurately out to 100 yards. Although it will never be as pinpoint accurate as a rifle, a slug barrel matched with proper loads makes it deadly. Most of these barrels run about 20-26 inches in length, and generally have rifle-type sights built in. The simple bead sight of a bird gun is a poor choice for deer hunting.

If your shotgun will accept one, consider buying a fixed low-power scope (2X) or a low-power variable (1–5X). There are many mount options for fixing scopes to shotguns. A good gunsmith can make suggestions for your particular gun.

Buckshot

Although a few states allow the use of buckshot for deer hunting, it is effective only at close range. If you use buckshot, try sizes 00 or 000. Take no shot beyond 30 yards. The larger the gauge, the better odds you'll have in making a clean kill, because the shell will carry more shot that will travel at a higher velocity. It is important to pattern your shotgun, just as you would for bird hunting, when using buckshot. Try several brands to see which one works best with your gun and choke combination.

Slugs

Most shotgun hunters use slugs. Two types are available. The Foster slug has been around a long time, and it has undergone improvements in recent years. This slug is essentially a round-nosed hunk of lead inscribed with rifling on its perimeter to cause it to spin as it travels down the barrel. This spin improves its accuracy.

More accurate, however, is the sabot-type (pronounced "say-bo") slug. It is an hourglass-shaped projectile encased in a plastic sleeve that peels away after exiting the barrel. For accuracy, this slug is generally preferred to the Foster type.

Test Fires

That said, it is possible your particular shotgun may prefer a Foster to a sabot. The only way to know for sure is to buy some of each (and perhaps a couple of brands of each) and test-fire them. Fortunately, most slug ammunition is available in boxes of 5 or 10 rounds, so it doesn't require a large outlay of cash to do the proper testing.

Just as you would when testing a rifle, shoot three-slug groups with the two types of slugs, and several brands, to see which one performs the best. Ideally, you should set the target at the maximum distance at which you would be comfortable taking a shot at a deer. Most slug ammunition will shoot relatively flat out to 50 yards, but begin to drop at 75. At 100 yards, most will have dropped by one-half to one inch—a drop not serious enough to ruin the chance of a clean kill. But beyond that distance, slugs lose their effectiveness. At about 125 yards, a Foster-type slug will no longer even have adequate energy for a clean kill on deer.

Shotguns are an extremely effective firearm for whitetails. You must, however, respect their limitations. In doing so, you'll be respecting your quarry as well.

Buckshot works well on deer at close range. Heavier loads are generally better than light ones, not because they increase your range, but because they give you a denser pattern.

Slugs include: (1) Sabot-type, which has a plastic sleeve that encases an elongated projectile and (2) Foster-style, which has a cup-shaped, nose-heavy design.

Muzzleloaders

Imagine a time when a firearm was not just something used recreationally for a week or two per year, but as a tool to put food on the table year-round. Such a firearm would need to be relatively foolproof and accurate.

That firearm was the muzzleloading rifle, perfected in the United States through trial and error. Early muzzleloading long guns were smooth bores—their barrels essentially no different inside than that of a shotgun. But with the advent of rifling, a leap in accuracy occurred.

This improvement meant hunters could take game at longer distances, but these guns had shortcomings. They were prone to misfire because of damp powder and hunters were relegated to a single shot.

Still, there is a romance to these guns and the skill it takes to handle them, which has led to great growth in modern muzzleloading, or "black powder" hunting. Many states and provinces now offer a primitive-weapons-only season.

Today, the term "muzzleloader" is used to describe everything from the traditional Hawkins-style rifle of our ancestors, to the modern in-line rifles.

Ignitions

Muzzleloaders come in three basic ignitions—flintlock, percussion (caplocks) and the modern "in-line" ignition, which is akin to the caplock.

The flintlock rifle does, indeed, use a piece of flint affixed to the hammer to create sparks in the frizzen to ignite the primer powder, which then ignites the main powder charge. Traditional caplock rifles look and work much the same as a flintlock, except that the hammer no longer contains flint, and the frizzen is replaced by a nipple over which a percussion cap is placed. When the hammer strikes the cap, it sends a flash through the nipple to ignite the charge. Caplocks are generally considered more reliable than flintlocks, and are faster in the sense that the main powder charge ignites more quickly than that of a flintlock.

Very popular are the newest black powder rifles, which have in-line ignitions. Looking much like a modern bolt-action rifle, these rifles use one of three types of caps to ignite the charge—the standard #11 cap, a "musket" cap (which produces more spark), or the 209 shotshell primer, the same primer used in many shotgun shells.

Flintlocks (above) have a flint in the hammer. When flint strikes frizzen, sparks ignite the primer powder and flame passes through a vent hole to set off the powder charge.

When the hammer of a percussion caplock (above) strikes a percussion cap, a flash travels through the nipple to ignite the powder charge.

The internal striker of an in-line percussion caplock (left) hits the cap on the nipple directly behind the powder charge, instantly setting it off.

Powder and Projectiles

All of these rifles still load via the barrel end, thus, are still muzzleloaders. Most hunters who use the two more traditional designs still opt to measure powder (which allows for both error, and custom loads). Many who choose the modern design employ an equally modern powder charge—pellets of powder that come in pre-measured sizes, usually of 50 grains each. Be sure to read the instructions for your rifle as some are rated up to 100 grains, while "magnum" black powder rifles can handle up to 150 grains.

True black powder is coded by coarseness of the grains—FFFg is the finest and used for priming flintlocks. Fg is the coarsest, and used for shotguns. Most rifles will perform best with either FFg (large caliber), or FFFg (small caliber).

Because black powder leaves a lot of corrosive residue, guns need a thorough cleaning after each use. To partially reduce the time needed for that chore, some hunters choose a black powder alternative called Pyrodex. Although Pyrodex is less expensive than black powder, and less corrosive, it is not as volatile—that is, it doesn't ignite quite as easily or burn as hot, leading some hunters to prefer the reliability of black powder, despite the need for cleaning. Two new black powder substitutes—Clean Shot and Triple Seven—are touted to be more volatile than Pyrodex, yet less corrosive.

Muzzleloading rifles come with varying amounts of rifling twist in their barrels, and the amount of twist often determines which type of projectile will work best with that rifle.

The most traditional rifles usually have a 1-in-60 twist (one full twist in 60 inches), and are best suited for round-ball projectiles. Some traditional guns in recent years have adopted a 1-in-48 twist, which still performs well with round balls, but will also allow the use of conical and sabot-type bullets. Most in-line rifles have a fast twist of about 1-in-32, which is great for conicals or sabots, but too fast for round balls, which become unstable.

Round balls are a short-range projectile, best suited for shots less than 50 yards, as they lose velocity more rapidly than the other two types of bullets. Sabot and conicals retain enough energy to kill a whitetail out to and sometimes beyond 100 yards.

Most deer hunters prefer a .50 or .54 caliber muzzleloader, but other options are available. Check your state's regulations to find out which calibers are legal. Also be advised that in many states, the addition of a telescopic sight is prohibited on muzzleloaders during muzzleloader-only seasons.

Finally, a few new black powder rifles now load through the breech with a bolt-like plunger, or break open like a double-barrel shotgun, and are loaded at that end. It is under debate whether these rifles truly qualify for use during primitive-weapon hunting seasons. Always check to learn what the area in which you plan to hunt allows.

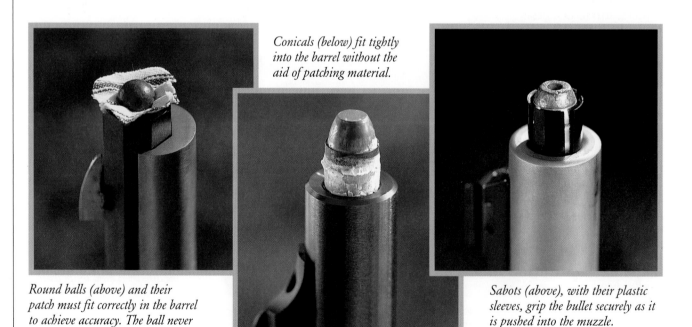

Conicals (below) fit tightly into the barrel without the aid of patching material.

Round balls (above) and their patch must fit correctly in the barrel to achieve accuracy. The ball never touches the inside of the barrel.

Sabots (above), with their plastic sleeves, grip the bullet securely as it is pushed into the muzzle.

Handguns for Whitetail Hunting

In the last twenty years or so, there has been a great increase in the use of handguns for hunting whitetails. While these hunters are only a small percentage of the total deer hunting population, their interest in this method has prompted the development of new handguns and loads.

Handgun hunting presents a challenge similar to bowhunting. Shots must be close, so the hunter needs skill in getting near deer, and must also practice long hours to become proficient. In addition, handguns allow many hunters with disabilities to participate in the firearms deer season—hunters who could not otherwise handle a rifle.

Types

Handguns that allow a two-handed hold—one on the pistol grip, the other on the gun's short forearm—can be shot more accurately than those that offer only a one-handed grip (or two hands, but near to each other). It isn't that these guns are inherently more accurate than the latter, but the wider hand "stance" tends to steady the shooter more. These longer barreled handguns also propel bullets with more energy than a shorter barreled gun of the same caliber, for the simple reason that the expanding gas stays with the bullet for a longer time as it travels down the barrel.

These types of handguns are usually single-shot pistols that either break open like a break-action shotgun, or actually have a bolt, like a rifle. Some of the bolt-action pistols hold more than one round. Many of these are chambered for short rifle cartridges, such as the .30-30 or the .35 Remington.

Revolvers are another popular choice, as they offer quick-repeat shots. However, they are limited to handgun calibers only, and even the most powerful possess less than half the energy of common rifle calibers. Popular choices for revolvers are the .454 Casull, .44 Remington Magnum and .41 Remington Magnum. Some may be tempted to use the .357 Remington Magnum and, in fact, in

some states it is legal to do so, but it really is an ineffective deer load.

Scopes and Accuracy

In order to improve your accuracy and to facilitate shots in low-light conditions, the addition of a pistol scope can be a great aid. Not only do these low-power scopes help the hunter to concentrate and hold on one spot, scopes gather light more effectively than the human eye and can make all the difference during that dawn or dusk hunt.

As with any deer hunting weapon, make sure you check the laws for the state in which you hunt. Some states do not allow scopes, and all states have restrictions on which caliber handguns you can use.

Because these large-caliber handguns do produce significant recoil, practice can be a painful affair. Many handgun hunters practice general accuracy by using a lighter caliber, but similar weight and configuration, handgun, then switch to their heavy hunting handgun a few weeks to a month before deer season. Practicing with the smaller caliber sharpens the eye and hones technique, but it is still necessary to shoot your hunting handgun—with the full loads you'll use for the hunt—to ensure that the skills you mastered with the other pistol transfer to your use of your hunting weapon.

Becoming proficient with a handgun is a very time-consuming task. Many hours of practice are required to achieve the consistent accuracy you need to make clean, ethical kills. If you are not willing to put in the time, then do not select a handgun as a hunting weapon.

Handguns for whitetail hunting include bolt-action repeaters (top), break-action single shots (center) and revolvers (bottom).

Archery Equipment

Longer seasons, less competition for hunting areas and the challenge of killing a deer at close range attract hunters to bowhunting. Archery equipment continues to be improved and refined, causing some hunters to bemoan technological intrusions to a primitive hunting method. Nevertheless, the modern bowhunter still relies on a stick and string, and must have the hunting skills necessary to get close enough to a deer for a shot.

When choosing a bow, it is best to seek advice at an archery specialty shop, because it is hard for a beginner to sort through the array of choices available. A hunter need not buy the most expensive equipment, but it does make sense to invest in high-quality gear.

Bow styles fall in three broad categories. Compound bows, which use cams and pulleys to transfer the energy to the limbs and reduce the effort needed to pull back the string, are used by the vast majority of deer hunters. Recurves and longbows are used by some hunters who enjoy the challenge of shooting with more traditional gear.

The amount of effort required to bend the limbs of a bow at full draw is called the draw weight. About 40 pounds is generally considered the minimum necessary to kill deer, but every state and province sets a minimum draw weight for hunting big game.

The draw length of an arrow varies with individuals. It is important to determine your nocking point, the place where you will hold an arrow at full draw. Some archers draw to touch their cheek, others touch their chin. What is most important is that your nocking point is consistent. The draw length is measured from the bottom of the nock groove to the far side of the bow.

Compound Bows

The mechanical advantage that reduces the effort needed to draw a compound bow is called let-off. The advantage of a compound's low holding weight is that archers can shoot a bow with a heavier draw weight and hold it at full draw while waiting for a shot. Although the Pope and Young record book for bowhunting trophies sets a maximum of 65 percent let-off for eligibility, many compounds have a let-off of 75 percent or more.

Compound cam configurations include the popular single cam, as well as cam-and-a-half or two-cam systems. The cam and wheels function like block and tackle to transfer energy to the limbs. The limbs of a compound bow are attached to the riser, which is where the grip, arrow rest, and sight are located. An adjusting bolt where the limb attaches to the riser allows you to change the draw weight.

Recurves and Longbows

Hunters who savor tradition shoot recurves or longbows. With both, the archer must hold the entire draw weight at full draw, so it requires hours of practice to develop muscle tone and become a proficient shot. Typical draw weights are 40 to 60 pounds.

The longbow has straight limbs and is the most traditional design, because it dates to the early days of archery hunting. The recurve, with its curved limbs, delivers more energy to the target.

Be aware that traditional bows (often called "stick" bows) are more difficult to use. They cannot be tuned and sighted with the same precision as compound bows.

Crossbows

Although they are not legal for deer hunting in very many places and often scorned by archers, crossbows are effective for killing deer. Designed with a short bow fixed horizontally on a stock, crossbows are fired with a trigger and may have a scope sight. In some places, they are allowed for hunters who have physical disabilities that prevent them from using standard archery gear.

Sights

Most archers use a sight. Typically, a peep embedded in the string is lined up with a pin on the riser that corresponds with the distance to the target. A wide variety of sights are available. Many incorporate fiber-optic material for better brightness in poor light conditions. Holographic and red-dot sights, incorporating technology developed for handguns, are also available.

Archers who do not use sights are called instinctive shooters, and usually are recurve or longbow shooters. Developing instinctive shooting skills requires significantly

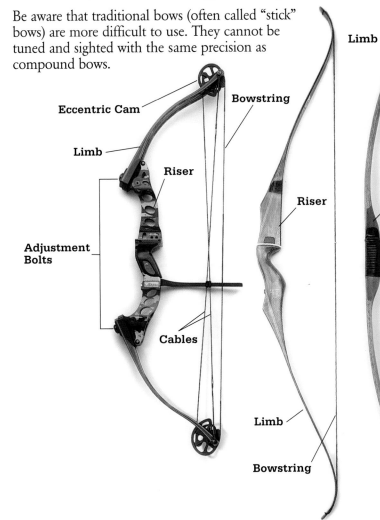

Bow types include compound bows (left), recurve bows (middle) and longbows (right). Compounds deliver the most energy for a given draw weight; longbows the least. A compound's limbs are of man-made materials. Recurves and longbows are usually made of fiberglass-wood laminates, though some longbows are solid wood.

Eccentric Cam

Bowstring

Limb

Riser

Riser

Adjustment Bolts

Cables

Limb

Bowstring

Limb

Riser

Bowstring

more practice than learning to shoot with a sight.

A sight system that is hard to see in low-light situations–early morning hours or in the shadows of a dense forest–is of little use. For this reason, bow-sight manufacturers are constantly developing and testing ways to improve visibility on sights.

Sights are especially valuable for beginners, because they make it easier to analyze mistakes. When shooting instinctively, it's hard to know if a miss is caused by bad form or a faulty aim, but with a sighting system, you'll know your aim is on target.

Whether you rely on simple pin sights or choose the latest in fiber-optic and laser-targeting technology, your selection is largely a matter of personal preference.

Releases

A mechanical release aid is used today by at least 75 percent of bowhunters to achieve a smooth, consistent release. The release is attached to a U-shaped loop on the bowstring and is released with a trigger device held in the archer's drawing hand.

Hunters who do not use a release, draw the string with two or three fingers. They use a leather tab or shooting glove to protect their fingers.

With practice, either method of arrow release can be successful, but the outcome of many hunts often comes down to one shot, and using a release aid can help make that shot count.

You can release your arrow using (1) a tab, (2) a leather shooting glove or (3) a mechanical release.

HHA Sports produces a full line of arrow rests (left, a fall-away model) and sights (right, a high-tech laser-type model).

Shaft types include (1) aluminum, (2) carbon and (3) wood.

Fletching types include feathers (top), which provide good stability, or plastic vanes (bottom), which are waterproof.

Arrows

Any bow must be matched with quality arrows to achieve the best performance. Arrow selection is based on draw weight, draw length, cam design, and the weight of the broadhead. All of your hunting arrows should be identical.

Small variations in length, diameter, head weight and fletching style can make it impossible to achieve consistent arrow flight.

Carbon is the most common shaft material, although some shooters use aluminum. Fiberglass or cedar arrows can be used with recurves and longbows. Many archers find wood arrows do not perform as consistently as aluminum or carbon.

The stiffness or "spine" of the shaft must be matched to the bow, or the arrow will fly erratically. Shaft diameter and weight, which affect penetration, are also important considerations when choosing hunting arrows.

Arrows are commonly fletched with three or four feathers or plastic vanes to give the arrow stability in flight. There are three common styles of attaching fletching to the arrow shaft: in a straight configuration, offset or in a helical pattern. You'll find feathers are wrapped left if they are left-wing feathers, or right if they are right-wing feathers.

An archery shop can help you select shafts that will perform well with your bow and suit your hunting needs.

Broadheads

Broadheads come in many styles, but all have one thing in common—they are razor sharp. Replaceable, fixed blades are popular. Fast-shooting bows are often matched with expandable broadheads which have retracted blades that expand on impact, because the arrows are traveling so fast that fixed blades affect flight. Old-style, fixed blades that are hand-sharpened are used by some traditional archers.

Regardless of broadhead style or size, precision is key for best flight. A broadhead acts as a wing on the front of an arrow, and if that wing is crooked, the arrow will fly erratically. Before using a broadhead on game, you can test its durability by shooting it into a foam 3-D target. If it doesn't perform well, try another style or brand until you feel comfortable that the penetration will be acceptable for a successful hunt.

Practice points should be the same weight as your hunting broadheads. They come in various diameters to match different-size shafts.

If you practice with broadheads, be sure to replace or sharpen the blades before you hunt. Regulations regarding legal broadheads vary, so make sure the ones you intend to use are legal where you hunt.

Among broadheads produced by Barrie Archery are the Snyper (top), the Tradition (middle) and the Ti100 (bottom).

Most states and provinces require a certain amount of blaze-orange clothing. Check the regulations in your area to be sure you're abiding by the law.

Clothing and Accessories

The clothing you wear for whitetail hunting should be suitable for the area of the country you live in, the temperature and weather patterns in your region, and whether you'll be hunting with a firearm or bow. But all clothing for deer hunting has a few things in common: It must be quiet, comfortable and durable. The most important thing to consider when purchasing accessories is to choose only those items necessary for safety and success.

Outerwear

Outerwear must be quiet. Deer have incredible hearing, and stiff fabrics that rustle when you move not only may spook deer, but make it difficult for you to hear them. Fabrics that are quiet include wool, fleece (and similar synthetics) and cotton. However, except for warm weather hunting, cotton is a poor choice because it too easily absorbs moisture, ruining its insulating qualities. In fact, in regions prone to wet, cool weather, cotton clothing can be downright dangerous since becoming chilled in these settings could lead to hypothermia—a sometimes fatal condition.

For those who walk to deer stands and then sit quietly for long periods in cold weather, outerwear should be packable. Wearing a heavy parka on the walk in will cause you to sweat, and once you stop, you will chill quickly. Carry a parka and pants or bibs of a high-lofting insulation such as down or polyester in a daypack.

Layering is an important component of keeping comfortable. The first layer against your skin should be of a wicking material. For quickly drawing perspiration away from the body, you can choose from silk, wool or synthetics like polypropelene and Thermax. Not only will this keep you more comfortable, it will help avoid hypothermia.

The next layer should also be of a material that allows perspiration to pass through. Fleece is again a good choice, as is wool. Each year it seems new fabrics with wicking capabilities are introduced, and many of these are available in pants and shirts. This layer also should be of a quiet material. Over this go your insulating coveralls or parka and pants.

In many locales, firearm hunters are required to wear blaze orange. Each state sets its own requirements, so become familiar with them. Some hunters who pursue whitetails in lightly hunted country may opt for natural-colored camouflage clothing over which they wear a blaze-orange vest. However, in places where hunting pressure is high, it is best to be safe and wear blaze orange from head to toe. Blaze-orange camouflage is also available and helps to break up your outline. While deer do not see color, they do seem to be able to more easily spot blaze orange because of its brightness, which camouflage helps to reduce. However, blaze camo is also less visible to other hunters. At least some part of your middle layer should also be blaze orange since you may want to strip down to that garment while walking to and from your stand, or while dragging out your deer.

In most places, bowhunters are not required to wear blaze orange unless hunting with a bow during the gun season. Most archers prefer camouflage. The pattern you use largely depends upon the habitat in which you hunt or the time of year.

Pursuing deer in a hardwood forest early in the autumn when foliage is still present would demand a different pattern than deer hunting in a pine forest or during late season when there is snow on the ground. For this reason, many hunters buy lightweight shell garments, each of a different pattern. These are worn over other clothing, and are an inexpensive way of building a wardrobe of camouflage patterns that can match any situation. Generally, camouflage patterns made up of large blocks of contrasting colors are more effective in breaking up your outline than patterns that are small and tight.

A trend has been toward clothing that is designed to control or eliminate human scent. Most of these garments contain a layer of odor-trapping carbon. In all cases, it is best to keep your deer hunting clothing clean and as odor free as possible. Washing it in a scent-free

detergent that contains no UV brighteners, then keeping it in a plastic bag until the hunt, is a good start.

It used to be that if it rained during a deer hunt, you were stuck either getting soaked, or wearing noisy raingear. Those days have ended. Several companies now offer raingear that is nearly as quiet as wool or fleece. The outer layer is a soft polyester material, and is usually bonded to Gore-Tex or some other breathable and waterproof membrane. While deer tend to restrict movement in a downpour, they actually move more often during periods of light rain or drizzle. These rain garments also help protect hunters who go afield during wet snowfalls, and they provide excellent protection from wind, which means you'll stay warmer.

Scent-Lok produces camouflage clothing that uses activated carbon to absorb odors and a moisture-wicking system to keep perspiration away from the skin.

CHOOSING CAMOUFLAGE PATTERNS

So why wear camouflage hunting clothes if whitetails don't see colors the same as you do? The answer may lie in the deer's ability to distinguish brightness.

Studies have shown that deer can assess brightness, although not as well as humans. What this means to hunters is that a camouflage pattern that uses large areas of dark and light colors for maximum contrast will best break up the human outline. Camouflage clothes with too "fine" a pattern appear to be a solid color when viewed from a distance. As a result, they lack contrast in brightness and are more easily seen by deer.

Be sure to choose camo for the season you will be hunting. Of course, the most important factor to avoid being spotted by deer is to remain motionless. While it is impossible never to move, you can hide much of your movement by leaving as much natural cover around you as possible.

Footwear

One of your most important clothing choices is footwear—and what you wear will obviously depend upon terrain and climate. Hunters in the North frequently wear pac boots—boots with a rubber bottom and leather or nylon tops—insulated with removable liners of wool felt, Thinsulate or other materials. These are wonderful boots for sitting in a blind or stand, but they are often awkward for walking long distances, and their large profile makes it difficult to walk quietly.

Boot makers also produce lighter weight pac boots, and build much warmer leather hunting boots. In some cases, these boots, when filled with 800 or more grams of these super-insulations, rival the warmth of heavy pac boots, yet are much better suited to walking.

Thinner soled boots are well suited to stalking. They are reasonably lightweight and waterproof, and give a good feel of the ground beneath your feet. Hunters who frequent rough, rocky terrain will do better with a lug-soled boot. In snake country, knee-high snake-proof boots might be a good option. Bowhunters often wear knee-high rubber boots to reduce scent.

Because wet feet mean cold feet, consider buying waterproof boots or Gore-Tex socks. The latter go over your regular socks, but are worn inside of any boot, providing excellent protection from the elements. Avoid wearing cotton socks, which soak up too much perspiration, leading to cold feet or blisters. A thin liner sock of polypropylene, olefin, or similar fabric is a great blister-proofing tool. Over that should go a sock of wool or synthetic material to provide warmth and cushioning.

Head and Hand Gear

Hats and gloves are important, not just for added warmth, but because they complete your camouflage wardrobe. The flash of a hand as you scratch your nose can be seen a long way off. Even bowhunters afield in hot weather often wear lighweight camo mesh gloves for just this reason. Cold-weather hunters should consider wearing a very lightweight liner-glove under heavy gloves or mittens. If the deer suddenly stops, and makes you wait after you have removed the warmer outer gloves–which happens often–the light liner-glove provides some protection to your hands as you wait for the shot.

Many hunters swear by the use of face masks and headnets, which not only help hide you, but can protect you from biting insects, and, in cold weather, offer added warmth.

Hats need to match your conditions. In hot weather, the lighter the better, and cold-weather hunters obviously will want an insulated hat. A brim helps shield you from the sun, reducing eyestrain.

Camouflage

In addition to wearing camouflage clothing, hunters also disguise their guns, bows and stands while hunting. Many hunting-related products now come in camo pattern finishes. Or, hunters may customize by adding camo tape or paint.

In warm weather, hunters often opt for face and hand paint over masks and gloves.

Many arrow manufacturers offer arrow shafts with camo paint.

Packs

You could easily double your own body weight with all the gadgets now available for hunters, many of which are unneeded. The best advice is to pack only what is necessary for safety and success.

Packs should be of a quiet material. Hunters can choose from many pack designs made of fleece or other quiet fabric, and even in a wide range of camouflage patterns or blaze orange.

Into that pack should go some things that are considered absolute essentials. These include:

• means of starting a fire (waterproof matches, disposable lighter or candle stub)

• map of the area

• emergency food such as jerky, chocolate or granola bars (in addition to your lunch)

• flashlight

• small first-aid kit

• compass (even if you also carry a GPS), which should always be carried on your person.

Other items that should be in your pack are:

• a drag rope

• some hunks of parachute cord for hoisting your gun or bow up into your tree stand

• toilet paper

• water

• disposable field-dressing gloves

• a couple of stout plastic bags to store the heart and liver

• moist towelettes for cleaning up after gutting your deer.

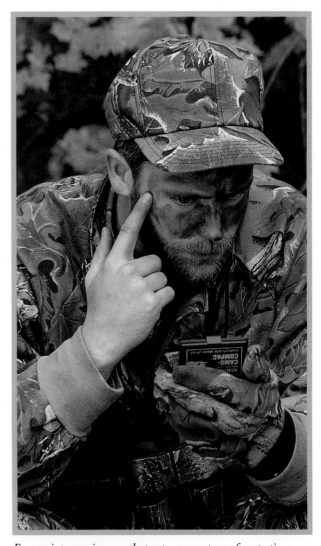

Face paint can give you that extra percentage of protection against a deer detecting your movement.

Optics

Binoculars are a great aid to deer hunters, even if you hunt in country where visibility is limited. Don't "check things out" through your rifle scope, since the thing you might be studying could be a person. Binoculars allow hunters not only to examine distant movement or terrain, but actually help see into the brush.

Don't buy cheap optics. It might be tempting to purchase those mini-binoculars; a mid-size pair is a better investment. They'll have a wider field of view, will gather light more efficiently, and are far easier to hold steady. The larger the objective end (the lens farthest from your eye), the better it will be for low-light situations. An 8x40 combination is a good place to start. Optics should be at least weather resistant, if not 100-percent waterproof.

If you wear eyeglasses, purchase a pair of binoculars with roll-down eyecups, and what is called "long eye relief." Together, these features will permit binocular use without having to remove your eyeglasses.

Compass

Always carry a good compass, and know how to use it. Some hunters even carry a spare in their pack. GPS (global positioning system) units are a very useful tool for finding your way around in the woods. They can also be used to plan your hunt or locate stands. Remember, however, that their batteries can run down. Compasses, when held level and away from your body and gun or equipment, are foolproof and dependable.

Good-quality binoculars are a must for any hunting situation. Manufacturers produce a variety of models in a wide range of prices, including Sightron SII WP 12x42 (1), Cabela's Big Sky 10x42 (2) and Zeiss Victory 12x56, BTP (3).

Knives for gutting whitetails include Gerber's Gator folding knife with a gutting hook (top), Browning's Buckmark fixed-blade knife (above) and Browning's three-bladed Field Dressing Tool (inset). Each has its advantages and the choice is yours, based on individual needs.

Knives

A knife for gutting a white-tailed deer need have a blade of only 3 to 6 inches long. Many fine sheath knives are available with blades of this length, as are many folding knives. Some have interchangeable (or multi-blade) designs, incorporating a small saw blade, which is not only handy for splitting a deer's pelvis, but for trimming limbs that might be in the way near your deer stand.

A drop-point knife—a style with a slightly blunted tip—is a better choice than those with a swept-up tip, since it'll be far less likely to puncture the deer's intestines during field dressing.

Another option is the Wyoming knife. Hunters who have used one say it opens game like a zipper and handles with speed, safety and efficiency. Whatever type of knife you choose, remember to always keep it razor-sharp.

Miscellaneous

There really are very few other things a hunter needs in the woods, but there are some items that you might want to consider.

• Chemical hand warmers are a nice touch in cold weather, and can also be considered a possible survival tool if you are forced to spend the night in the cold deer woods.

• A space blanket is another good thing to have if you find yourself spending a night in the woods. Most models roll up into a very small package and it can be a life saver.

• A small camera for capturing memories of days afield.

• An extra pair of dry socks, though not a necessity, can really make the second half of a full day's hunt much more pleasant.

• Some kind of seat—whether a soft, quiet pad you place on the ground or on a five-gallon bucket, a folding stool or a seat that clamps to a tree—can add immeasurably to the length of time you can sit quiet and motionless.

CHAPTER THREE

Preparing for the Hunt

Many deer-hunting stories begin with that split second it takes for a shot to hit home. But most successful hunts begin much earlier, sometimes more than a year in advance. Doing a little research will help to make the best use of your time afield and improve your odds of taking a deer.

Gathering Information

A wealth of information is available to help you find good places to hunt. Start with a copy of state or provincial hunting regulations to learn about seasons, legal methods and bag limits. Natural resource agencies also have web sites that show public hunting opportunities, deer population and harvest statistics, and other pertinent information. If you are traveling to hunt, a web search will help you find guides and outfitters. Whenever possible, try to talk with individuals who have hunted in the area previously, such as friends, co-workers or members of your local sportsman's club.

As your search narrows for potential hunting areas, gather maps. Excellent maps are available on the Internet or as software. You can also get free or inexpensive maps of state and federal public lands. Statewide county atlases, sold at bookstores, are invaluable. The best maps show topographic detail, including land contours, wetlands, roads and trails, and vegetation types. Aerial photos, which are updated regularly, give you a bird's-eye view of actual terrain. A plat book, showing the individual properties and landowners for a local area, is published by each county.

Helpful sources of local information are wildlife managers, foresters and conservation officers. You should be able to locate their telephone numbers on natural resource agency web sites or by calling the public information number listed in hunting regulations booklets. Don't expect wildlife professionals to tell you exactly where to hunt—most don't want to concentrate hunting pressure—but they will give you information about deer populations, hunter access, hunter success and terrain. In some situations, they

Topographical maps provide information on land elevation and detail features of the landscape, such as wetlands. They also show buildings, roads and trails.

Shed hunting in the spring can give clues to what bucks may still be in the area after last season's hunt.

For most hunters, the hardest part of taking any deer, including a trophy buck, is getting permission to hunt the land it calls home. Thousands of acres of private land in North America—small farms, huge ranches, broken suburban lots and bordering crop fields—are closed to hunting. Hundreds of bucks live within such sanctuaries, safe from human predators.

How do you find such places? Just look for the signs. Posted. No Hunting. No Trespassing. Listen for rumors flying around town about the huge buck seen crossing a certain road. Ask at the local cafe and gas station. Who's been seeing big bucks? Who got the big bucks last year? Call these folks and get friendly with them. Join the local hunting club and exchange information. If you hear about a big buck on private land, make it your goal to gain access where no one else is allowed.

Your first strategy may be to take up the bow. Archers are often welcomed in places closed to gun hunters. Second, get to know the landowners. Don't be shy and don't let the "No" signs frighten you. Many farmers post their property just to keep from being pestered, or to cover themselves against frivolous lawsuits. If you know who owns a piece of hot property, make a phone call or drive out for a visit. If you don't know the owner, check county plat maps or ask around at the local co-op or farm-equipment retailer.

When you visit the landowner:

• Be open, honest and friendly.

• Tell the landowner you're always looking for a beautiful, quiet place to hunt, where you can get away from the crowds and enjoy nature.

• Tell him you're after mature bucks only and have no interest in shooting fawns or females

(unless the landowner wants you to remove a doe for management reasons).

• Mention that you hunt by yourself and want the challenge of hunting the smartest buck in the countryside.

• Offer to help the farmer with his evening chores as payment for the right to hunt on his property.

If he turns you down, respect his reasons, but try to counter them tactfully if you can. Many landowners post their land because they've had bad experiences with inconsiderate hunters. Here are some additional things you can discuss:

• Assure him you won't drop litter, start fires or leave gates open.

• Offer to park in his yard while you hunt.

• Give him your hunting license number.

• Provide character references from other farmers and respected locals.

If the landowner still says no, thank him as you leave, but keep his name and address in your files. Several months later, send him a Christmas card or a brief note describing your latest hunting season. Try again the following year. Polite persistence sometimes wears down resistance.

Another strategy is to ask permission simply to take photographs or look for antlers on the property. If a friendship or mutual respect blossoms, you can later ask for permission to hunt.

In essence, you are "courting" the landowner or farmer. If you show a genuine interest in him as a person and can convey a sincere love of the outdoors and respect for his land, your chances are good for winning him over. In the end, you may find that making new friends only improves you as a hunter.

may direct you to private landowners who are experiencing problems with deer and are looking for responsible hunters to reduce their numbers.

To locate accommodations, campgrounds and local services, contact the state or provincial tourism office for area listings. Use the Internet to find individual businesses and make inquiries or reservations. A call to the local chamber of commerce will help you find lodging and may lead to new sources of information.

If you are hunting in another state or province, begin researching a year or more in advance of the hunt so you can meet deadlines for nonresident license applications or apply for special hunts. Hunting outfitters are often fully booked for a year or more. You will also want to find out if nonresidents are required to have a hunter safety certificate from their home state.

When gathering information, ask about the weather during hunting season, hunting pressure, special clothing needs and necessary gear. Make clothing and equipment purchases well in advance of the hunt so you have time to make sure that the clothes fit and your gear is in working order. If the hunting season lasts a week or more, ask how hunting conditions change as it progresses. When planning to hunt on private land, secure permission or pay access fees well in advance of your hunt.

If you seek a high-quality hunt, look for special seasons held before or after the general firearms season. Many places have lightly hunted, early archery or late muzzleloader seasons. Areas with exceptionally high deer numbers may hold special hunts intended to reduce deer numbers. Ask, too, about the timing of the rut and seasonal deer movements. Whitetails may change their patterns as they adapt to hunting pressure or the weather.

Trophy buck hunters must put extra effort into information gathering. Ask specific questions about local entries into record books, differences between trophy potential on public and private lands, and any recent trends in weather or hunting pressure that could affect overall numbers of mature bucks. When shopping for a guide or outfitter, ask for hunter success rates and always get references from previous clients.

Scouting

The primary tool used by successful deer hunters is scouting. There is no substitute for time spent in the field. Avid hunters visit their hunting area throughout the year, so they become familiar with the land and the deer living there. They learn about seasonal deer movements, food sources, local population abundance, good stand locations, human use of the land and a myriad of details that become part of a successful hunting strategy.

The size of the area you scout is determined by things like the amount of property where you have permission to hunt, use by other hunters, and your personal hunting style. When scouting a new area, first learn the lay of the land. Use a topographic map and compass to locate property lines, roads, trails, water courses and prominent natural features. A handheld GPS (Global Positioning System) can be used to log-in specific locations for future reference. Bright-colored, plastic surveyor's tape can be tied to branches and saplings to mark forest paths and stand sites. On private land, be sure you have the landowner's permission to use the tape or other marking material. And on public land, be sure to remove the tape after your hunt.

Your first priority is to look for deer sign, the evidence that whitetails use the area. Hoofprints, droppings, trails, beds, rubs, scrapes and browsed twigs are sign you may encounter while scouting. A good hunter becomes a student of deer sign and what it reveals about the local deer population. Generally, deer sign is easiest to find during fall and winter, and more difficult to see in dense, summer foliage. In summer, you may learn more about

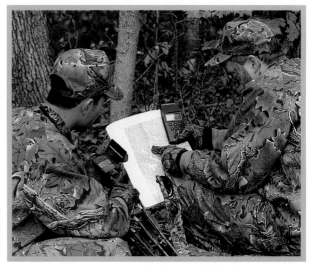

Using a GPS unit, along with a map of your hunting area, can help make scouting more productive.

the deer in your hunting area by watching for them in fields where they feed at dawn and dusk.

Pre-season

Always try to start scouting at least a couple of weeks prior to your planned hunt. Look for trails the deer use when moving through the area. In farm country, you may find distinct feeding areas, such as crop fields and dense cover used as a bedding area. Trails leading between these two locations are excellent places to hunt. In large forested areas, deer movements may seem more random. Look for frequently used trails and edges between dense forest cover, such as conifers, and more open hardwoods.

In areas where deer habitat is limited by agricultural activity, residences and development, or land features, look for funnel spots that the deer must pass through when traveling from one cover to another. These are usually good stand locations. Be aware that you may find places with lots of deer sign, but little security or nearby escape cover. These locations are typically visited by whitetails at night and avoided during the day. Pay attention to prevailing winds, so that you can plan ways to enter your hunting area

by walking upwind or crosswind. Make note of places that are sheltered from winds, because the deer will use them on windy or stormy days.

The Rut

Mating activity occurs from early autumn, when bucks begin polishing their antlers, into winter, when the does finish their estrous cycles. Initially, you'll see small saplings with shredded bark and broken branches made by bucks rubbing their antlers. As the mating season nears, you'll begin to see small scrapes along deer trails. The early rutting evidence is often misleading, because the buck that made it may establish a territory elsewhere during the rut.

Buck sign is prominent for about three weeks in autumn at the height of the rut. This is when you'll find large scrapes and sparring rubs. Fresh rut sign often means a buck is nearby. If you are hunting for bucks during the rut, scout within a few days of when you plan to hunt. Then, during the hunt, continue looking for fresh rutting activity. When you locate an area that is being used by a buck, plan a hunting strategy that will create minimal disturbances.

Deer sign to look for when scouting include: evidence of deer feeding on corn cobs or browsed twigs (right), rubs on trees (far right, top), groups of deer droppings (far right, bottom), clusters of scrapes, trails and beds (opposite page, left to right).

Hunt and Scout

During the hunting season, scout for recent deer activity and new places to hunt. You can combine scouting with a still-hunt. Pay attention to details, such as the points from which other hunters enter your hunting area and where their stands are located. Then look for places where the deer go to avoid other hunters. Plan your hunting strategy accordingly. Even on heavily hunted public lands, you may find places infrequently visited by other hunters that are used as escape cover by deer. A physical barrier such as wet ground or dense foliage may make it difficult to enter these areas, but extra effort may pay off with a successful hunt.

Whitetail activity is affected by the availability of food. Learn to identify and locate the fall foods whitetails prefer in your hunting area. After killing frosts, deer in the forest shift from eating vegetative matter to woody browse. In agricultural areas, feeding patterns are associated with crop harvests. The abundance of natural foods, such as acorns, varies from year to year, and your hunting strategy may change accordingly.

Post-season

Scouting after the season is over can be very helpful. Early-winter deer movements are usually similar to those used in the recently ended hunting season. The most significant difference is that the bucks are no longer in rut. Look for sign from the rut, such as scrapes and rubs, and mark where you find it. Very likely, rut activity will occur in the same place the next year.

Later in the winter and in spring, you can look for antlers shed by bucks. Many folks find shed-antler hunting an enjoyable way to scout and spend time in the woods. Focus your search on winter cover such as conifer stands, south-facing slopes and feeding areas. Walk slowly, scanning the ground around you for the telltale shape of an antler or an upright tine. If you find one antler, carefully search the surrounding area for a radius of 50 yards or more. You may find the other.

If you are lucky enough to find several antlers, you may learn something about antler sizes and the age-classes of bucks in your area. Finding a trophy-size antler can fuel your dreams, because the buck that dropped it may still be around next year.

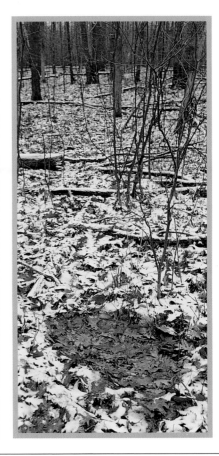

Sighting-in and Shooting Firearms

Deer hunters must be competent with the guns they use for hunting–whether rifle, shotgun, muzzleloader or handgun. Being a good shot is not a birthright, nor is it a skill acquired through casual study. Shooting a few rounds prior to the hunt to make sure your gun is sighted-in is not sufficient practice to know that you can make the shot when a deer steps out. If you want to shoot well, you must practice until you are confident that you can hit what you're shooting at under field conditions.

Finding a place to shoot is a challenge for many hunters as urban sprawl and local ordinances lead to the closure of both shooting ranges and informal shooting places like gravel pits. Find a place to shoot long before hunting season begins so you have sufficient time for practice. To find nearby shooting ranges, you can simply check the Yellow Pages, or you can contact local law enforcement representatives, conservation department offices or the National Shooting Sports Foundation (www.nssf.org). These sources will know of ranges operated by a sportsman's club, the state conservation department or a private owner. Most ranges allow you to shoot for a small fee or the price of a membership. If you own or have access to rural property, you can set up your own shooting range.

At the range, shooting distances should be defined for 10, 25, 50, 100 and 200 yards so you can sight-in and practice with hunting guns. The range may provide bench rests, targets and other amenities. A range officer oversees the area and is responsible for safety. Be sure you understand and follow the range rules.

Know Your Gun

Before you go to the shooting range, learn how your gun functions. With the gun unloaded, become familiar with the sights, the safety, the action and the magazine. Perform a cleaning disassembly. If you want to try dry-firing–practicing pulling the trigger with an unloaded gun–get a snap cap, which allows the firing pin to make a strike without damaging the spring.

All guns work on the same principal. Igniting gunpowder causes an explosion that propels a projectile–called a bullet or a slug–down the barrel, launching it toward a target. Generally, bullets used for deer hunting travel at speeds ranging from 1,000 to over 3,000 feet per second, which means that they reach the target in an instant. In the course of flight, a bullet must counter the effects of gravity, which pulls it toward the ground. To

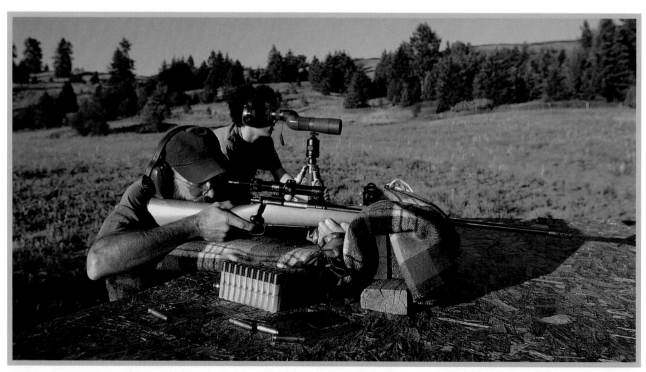

Sighting-in your firearm is important, whether you shoot with rifle (above), shotgun, muzzleloader or handgun.

compensate for gravitational pull, the bullet travels at a slight arc, which is called trajectory. The relationship between bullet speed and trajectory is called ballistics.

Study the ballistics information for the ammunition you intend to use while hunting. For factory-loaded ammunition, this information may be available on the cartridge box or in a manufacturer's brochure. Knowing the trajectory, measured in inches at specific distances, will help you select the proper ammunition and sight-in your gun. A selection of ammunition or loads is available for most calibers. If you are uncertain which load is best for your gun, seek advice from an experienced shooter or hunter. Gun stores have knowledgeable staff who can answer your questions.

Sighting-in Firearms

Sight-in your gun prior to every hunting season. If you travel a long distance, take a few shots before you hunt to make sure the gun is still sighted-in. If you accidentally jar the gun during a hunt (perhaps by falling down, or dropping the gun), or if you inexplicably miss a deer, shoot at a target to again check for accuracy.

Firearms should be kept clean, dry and in a protective case when not in use. Begin the sighting-in process by giving the gun a once-over to make sure that scope mounts are tight; look for any visible damage, and check the tightness of all screws and bolts. If the rifle has never been sighted-in, use a bore-sighting tool to make initial scope adjustments.

Use targets with a bull's-eye at least 3 inches in diameter. A 6-inch bull's-eye is easier to see. Begin the sighting-in process with the target placed at 25 yards. At that distance, all bullets are still on the rise of trajectory. When zeroed at 25 yards, most rifles will shoot about 2 inches high at 100 yards and return to zero at about 200 yards. Muzzle-loaders, shotguns and handguns, which have projectiles traveling at slower speeds, have a shorter range, but the trajectory principle is the same.

Always fire sighting-in rounds from a solid resting position. Ideally, you should use sandbags to steady your firearm on a bench rest, though you can also use cushions to rest the gun. With open sights or a scope, aim exactly where you want the bullet to strike the target. Keeping the same sight picture for each shot, fire three rounds. Then check the target. Your shots should form a group and indicate where the gun is aiming. Make sight or scope adjustments if necessary and fire three more rounds.

Some tips for sighting-in your firearm include: Adjust your scope by turning the horizontal or vertical adjuster screws (right). Cover each 3-shot group with tape before making adjustments and firing another group; this will prevent you from becoming confused by too many bullet holes in the same target (below, left). Sight-in with the same load you use for hunting; different-weight bullets impact in different spots on a target (below right).

When you are satisfied that the gun is sighted-in, move the target to a longer distance–50 yards for shotguns and handguns, 100 yards for muzzleloaders and rifles. Fire three-shot groups, which should strike 1 to 3 inches higher on the target due to rising trajectory. Make any necessary horizontal adjustments.

If your gun shoots inconsistent groups, try different ammunition. Many guns are more accurate with specific loads. If you remain unsatisfied with the accuracy, ask an experienced shooter to try the gun. If he or she gets the same result, the accuracy problem may be the gun or sights, and you should visit a gun shop or gunsmith for further advice.

Sight-in with the ammunition you intend to use for hunting. You can shoot less-expensive rounds for general target practice. Read shooting magazines and consult ballistics tables to select your hunting loads. For rifles, use bullets designed for deer-size animals. A common myth is that heavier bullets "bust brush" better than lighter ones. In reality, all bullets may deflect when they strike a twig or stem.

Once your gun is sighted-in, spend some time shooting it. Remember, sighting-in is done from a controlled setting such as a bench rest to make the gun accurate–a process that doesn't necessarily make you a better shot. Practice from the various shooting positions until you're confident that you can hit a dinner plate, which is about the size of a deer's vital areas, on every shot.

Distance Shooting

Every firearm has an acceptable range for making consistent, killing shots. Most handgun and shotgun hunters try to keep their shots within 50 yards, though some guns and loads–in the hands of an experienced shooter–are capable of greater distances. Black powder shooters limit their shots to about 100 yards, again with some exceptions.

Rifles are capable of greater distances, though just how far is dependent upon the caliber and the load. The venerable .30-30 is best at ranges of less than 150 yards. A .270 can reach out to 300 yards or more. In most of the whitetail's range, nearly all hunting shots are taken at distances of 200 yards

or less. Many expert hunters strongly recommend that even if your rifle is capable of greater distances, hunting shots should be confined to 300 yards or less.

The longer the shot, the more variables come into play. First, you must accurately judge the distance. A range finder or range-finding scope is useful, especially if you are not experienced at making long shots in the field. With a flat-shooting rifle, you should be able to aim directly at the vitals out to 200 yards. But as distances increase, you must account for trajectory. If there is a breeze, you must also consider bullet drift.

Stories abound of whitetail hunters who make a Western hunting trip and are stymied by the long shots typical of open country. If you plan to hunt in the West, be sure you spend plenty of practice time at the shooting range before you go. Buy a range finder and learn not only how to use it, but also to become reasonably adept at judging distances. Preparation always pays off–no matter where you hunt.

Common Shooting Positions

Whenever possible, shoot from a resting position with the gun steadied by an inanimate object, such as the railing on a tree stand. In hunting situations, however, you don't always have the opportunity to shoot from a rest. It is essential to know how to fire from the basic shooting positions: prone, sitting, kneeling and offhand. You can take shooting instructions or a gun safety class to learn more about these positions.

• Prone is the steadiest position. It is most useful in open country, where the deer is some distance away and you are able to lie down and shoot. Lie on your stomach with your body tilted at a 30-degree angle from the line of fire. The butt of the gun forms the apex of the angle. Spread your legs apart for support. Use your elbow to support the forearm of the gun. The elbow of your trigger hand should rest on the ground.

• The sitting position is nearly as steady as the prone position and more practical in some field situations. Sit with the lower half of your torso at a 30-degree angle from the line of fire. Spread your legs apart and rest your elbows on your knees. Some shooters prefer to sit with their ankles crossed.

• The kneeling position can be used when brush or high grass obscure the view from sitting or prone positions. Kneeling is less steady and many shooters find it a difficult position to assume. Kneel with the knee on the same side of your body as your trigger hand. Sit back on that foot and ankle. Slide your other foot forward and rest the elbow of the arm supporting the gun's forearm on the knee.

• Offhand is the least steady position, but is often used when you have just a few moments to make the shot. It can also be described as a freestanding position. Stand with your feet apart and your body leaning slightly toward the line of fire. Tuck the elbow of the arm supporting the forearm beneath the gun. Raise the elbow of your trigger hand until it is horizontal. Practice shooting from this position until you are confident you can hit targets at typical deer-hunting distances.

Commonly used shooting positions include: sitting (far right, top), kneeling (far right, center), off-hand (far right, bottom), using a solid rest (above) and prone (right).

FIREARMS SAFETY

It is your responsibility to always follow safe gun-handling rules. You can avoid accidents when you're in the field by keeping these tips in mind:

• Always be aware of where your barrel is pointing. Around other hunters, keep the barrel pointed up. When you load a firearm, stand away from other hunters with the barrel pointed toward the ground.

• Don't use your gun scope to look at distant hunters.

• Some lever-action rifles commonly used for deer hunting, as well as some other firearms, have exposed hammers that are cocked and must be uncocked if the gun isn't fired. Step away from other hunters and point the gun toward the ground when you uncock it. Use firm thumb pressure on the hammer and ease it forward as you squeeze the trigger.

• Most lever-action guns have a safe, half-cock position. In the fully uncocked position, the hammer rests against the firing pin mechanism and, if jarred, the gun may go off.

• Always leave your safety on until you are ready to shoot. Get in the habit of checking frequently to make sure your safety is on as you hunt. If you shoot at a deer, make sure to put the safety back on before you move.

• Unload your gun before climbing into a tree stand, crossing a fence or jumping a creek. Also unload it when you take a lunch break with other hunters or quit hunting for the day. Keep the action open, so everyone (including you) knows the gun is unloaded.

• Carry only the ammunition that you will use in your firearm so you won't mistakenly load it with different ammo.

• Be certain of your target and what is behind it before taking a shot. Take your time and aim carefully. A rushed shot is a poor shot.

Portable Rests

Shooting with a steady gun can mean the difference between a hit and a miss. Awkward positions can be greatly improved by using a steadying tool. Here are three suggestions.

• The sling is most often used to carry a gun and leave your hands free. Some shooters use a sling to become more steady in all shooting positions. The sling goes around the outside of the arm used to steady the gun. Adjust the sling to fit you. When beginning a hunt, check the adjustment to make sure the sling fits with your bulkier hunting clothes.

• Folding shooting sticks are carried in a belt pouch and used to steady the gun, often from a sitting position. The sticks are crossed to form an X. The forearm rests in the apex.

• Bipods are attached to the forearm and folded up when not in use. Open-country hunters find them especially useful for prone and sitting shots. A telescoping monopod is lightweight and can be used for sitting and standing shots.

Tips for steady shooting include using a sling (top) when a solid rest is not available; and becoming adept at using a bipod (above).

Tuning and Shooting Bows

Killing a deer with a bow and arrow is an achievement. You must first master the skills of archery and then learn to hunt well enough to get close to whitetails. Typically, bowhunters spend more time in the field, because it is difficult to get within arrow range of a deer. When you do, you get just one shot.

Becoming a competent archer requires lots of practice. Fortunately, it is easy to find places to shoot. Many hunters are able to set up a target with a safe backstop in their backyards. Archery ranges exist in many communities. Indoor ranges are available for year-round shooting.

Consistency

The motions of drawing and releasing an arrow come naturally for most of us. The challenge is acquiring the consistency to make the same motion time and again in a variety of conditions so you can reliably hit a plate-size target at typical hunting distances. Archers develop individual styles, but they practice until the steps of draw, anchor, sight, release and follow-through become second nature. Consistency leads to accuracy.

When practicing, pay attention to shooting position. Find a comfortable upper-body stance and stick with it whether you are standing, kneeling or sitting in a tree stand. To shoot at various angles, learn to bend at the waist. Hold the bow lightly, because a tight grip affects arrow flight.

The anchor point, which is where your string hand holds the arrow at full draw, must be the same on every shot. Varying the anchor point changes the course of the arrow. To hold a consistent anchor point, many archers touch their chin, cheek or the corner of the mouth with their index finger or mechanical release on every shot. Find the anchor point that feels right for you and stick with it.

A smooth release leads to accuracy. Practice finger or mechanical releases to avoid moving or plucking the string. Focus on your aim, so that the release occurs when you are confident that you are on target. Then you won't hesitate when taking a shot at a whitetail. Remain steady after the release so the arrow flies true.

For accuracy and success, correct shooting form requires proper body position and correct hand positions.

Sighting Methods

Today many archers use bowsights to improve their accuracy. If you are skilled at judging range, sights will help you achieve consistent accuracy. Instinctive shooters don't use sights, but instead rely on experience to place their shots.

Set sight pins for the distances you are most likely to shoot while hunting. To sight-in a bow, move the pin opposite of the direction you expect the arrow to go. For instance, if you are shooting low, move the pin lower. Practice until you can draw and then hold until you release.

Instinctive shooting requires more practice, but is really no different than learning how to throw a ball. Draw and release when the shot feels right. Focus on the target. Some shooters use the point of the arrow as a guide. Practice frequently to hone instinctive skills.

Whether using sights or a bare bow, begin practicing at 10 yards and move back in 5-yard increments as your shooting improves. The distance at which you can consistently hit a pie plate is your effective hunting range.

Practice Techniques

Use target points for practice at block targets or bales. If your practice area is in the backyard or close to home, remember that it is better to take a few shots often than to have an occasional long practice session. Remember, you'll only get one shot when hunting.

Large archery ranges may have a walk-through area where you can shoot at game-size targets in realistic field conditions. You can get similar practice by stump-shooting. Find a place where you are unlikely to meet other people and shoot at stumps or other objects at varied distances. Use judo points, which stop rapidly in grass or forest duff so your arrows are easy to find. Don't shoot at hard objects such as rocks or tree trunks, which may damage your arrows or cause ricochets. Bowhunting for rabbits or other small game during the off-season is excellent practice for deer hunting.

It is a good idea to practice while wearing your hunting clothes so you know that they won't interfere with your shooting. Take shots from a tree stand and a ground blind. Shoot from varied positions, including crouched, kneeling and sitting. If

Shoot arrow groups at the exact distance of your sight's top pin to determine if the pin is correctly aligned. If the arrow groups (red dots) are off-center, move the pin. Shoot several arrow groups, adjusting the pin until the arrows hit where the pin is positioned. As the arrow leaves the bow, your hands and arms should hold the same position and your bow should move very little. Once your arrow has hit the target (or deer), then you can lower the bow to see where it has hit.

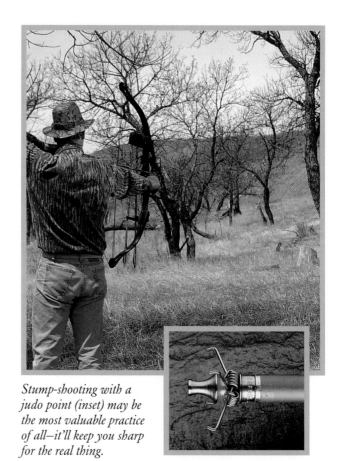

Stump-shooting with a judo point (inset) may be the most valuable practice of all—it'll keep you sharp for the real thing.

you hunt in open country, practice on windy days.

Prior to going hunting, take some shots with your broadheads, which fly differently than target points. Be sure you have a solid backstop, such as a pile of clean sand. Carefully examine arrows and sharpen the broadheads afterward, so they are ready for the hunt.

Tuning a Bow

Adjusting a bow to fit you and achieve good arrow flight is called tuning. You can learn how to make the proper adjustments from your bow's owner manual or at an archery shop. Establish your draw length and the bow's draw weight. Use a bow square to set a nocking point. Place silencers on the string to minimize the chance a deer will "jump the string" when you release a hunting shot.

Test arrow flight by shooting through a taut sheet of paper placed 10 feet away. A straight-flying arrow will cut an even fletching pattern. An odd-shaped pattern means the arrow is wobbling in flight. Adjust first the nock point and then the arrow rest to improve performance. Step back to 30 feet and shoot the paper again. Make any necessary adjustments.

Using field points, test your hunting arrow shafts by shooting at a mid-range target. Try to keep the arrows in a tight group. Mark arrows that don't stay in the group and shoot again. Don't use inconsistent arrows for hunting. Never try to shoot groups with broadheads, because you may cut fletchings or damage shafts.

By tuning your bow and making performance tests, you'll gain confidence in your equipment and your ability as an archer. Now you are ready to go hunting!

ARCHERY SAFETY

• Carry your arrows in a quiver that covers the broadheads.

• Never walk with a nocked arrow.

• Never dry-fire a compound bow—or any bow for that matter. Not only could you damage it, but you could snap a limb or break a string, causing injury to yourself or a bystander.

Shot Placement for Bullet, Slug and Arrow

A good deer hunt ends with a humane, one-shot kill. If your shot strikes the vitals, the animal dies quickly, which makes it easier for you to recover the deer. Understanding whitetail anatomy is essential to shot placement, because you don't always get a perfect shooting opportunity. Whitetails may approach you from any direction, never stop moving, and be partially obscured by vegetation. Learn to identify the vital area from various angles. Practice shooting until you are able to shoot quickly and with confidence.

The primary vital area consists of the heart, lungs and liver, located in the chest cavity behind the front shoulder. The neck contains major blood vessels and several vertebrae. A whitetail's brain is relatively small. Breaking the backbone will incapacitate the deer, but is unlikely to kill it.

A heart/lung shot is best, because the chest cavity is the largest target. The proximity of the liver and spine allows some margin of error. An open, broadside shot is preferred, but learn to identify the heart/lung area from various angles. The bone structure, including the shoulder, may cause your shot to deflect.

While neck and head shots may result in quick kills, both are risky targets. A near-miss may wound or maim the animal, but not be serious enough to prevent its escape. Every hunting situation is different and on occasion you may be compelled to shoot at the head or neck. Take the shot only if you are certain you will hit where you aim.

A deer bounding directly away from you generally doesn't offer a shooting opportunity unless it is wounded and you are trying to put it down. If you must make such a shot, aim beneath the white tail. Conversely, if a deer is walking directly toward you, it may be best to wait for the animal to turn and present a better, quartering shot. Do not shoot if a second deer is standing behind the deer you intend to kill, because bullet, slug or arrow may pass through the deer and hit the other animal.

Bullets and slugs kill with tissue damage and associated trauma. Use a bullet designed for hunting

Ground-level shots tend to be the most successful—broadside (left) exposes 100% of the deer's heart/ lung area; quartering toward (below left), 65%; quartering away (below middle), about 60%; and head-on (below right), 35%.

Steep-angle shots tend to be less successful, with quartering toward (above left) and quartering away (above middle) exposing 55% of the deer's vital area. Walking away (above right) exposes about 45%.

deer-size animals, which expands as it enters the body. Factory-made ammunition suitable for deer hunting is widely available.

Arrows kill by slicing and creating hemorrhage. Select broadheads designed to make cutting wounds. An arrow that penetrates the heart/lung area will kill as quickly and efficiently as a bullet.

Safety

Years ago, hunting accident rates were much higher than they are today, even though there were significantly fewer hunters. The advent of mandatory hunter safety programs for young hunters and voluntary training for adults has made hunting one of the safest recreational activities. Nevertheless, preventable accidents still occur. You can take precautions to ensure the safety of yourself and other hunters.

Deer hunting is a strenuous physical activity. Be physically prepared to walk on uneven terrain, climb into tree stands and drag out a deer. Wear foot gear with ankle support to prevent sprained ankles. Even if it is warm during the day, have sufficient clothing to remain warm if the temperature drops. Carry water and food.

Never go afield without basic gear that will allow you to meet situations you may encounter afield. Have a reliable means for starting a fire, such as waterproof matches. A small candle will help you start a fire even in wet conditions. Carry a flashlight, a length of rope, a knife and gloves.

A GPS unit is a handy tool, but you should also carry a compass and know how to use it. Take out the compass at your starting point and determine what direction you will need to go to get out of the woods. For instance, if you walk west from a road running north and south, walking east will bring you back to the road.

It is hard to get lost in most whitetail hunting areas, but it may be difficult to find your way in unfamiliar country or after darkness falls. Be sure to tell someone where you are going and when you plan to return. Pay attention to natural features and landmarks. Above all, don't fear the forest or panic if you lose your way. If night falls and you don't know where you are, stop, gather firewood, build a fire and wait for someone to come looking for you. If you are in good physical condition, at worst you'll spend an uncomfortable night in the woods.

Treat every gun as a loaded weapon. And when hunting with bow and arrow, remember that broadheads are razor-sharp and can easily inflict life-threatening cuts or puncture wounds.

Wearing some amount of blaze-orange clothing is required for most firearms deer hunts. Be sure you know the guidelines in the state or province where you hunt. Although some hunters believe whitetails can distinguish the brightness of the color, hundreds of thousands of whitetails are killed annually by orange-clad hunters. Wear as much blaze orange as you believe is necessary for other hunters to easily see you. Blaze-orange camouflage patterns, though somewhat less visible, can be worn to break up your outline.

Bowhunters usually are not required to wear blaze orange. Typically, they wear camouflage to blend in with the surroundings. If you are hunting in an area where small game or turkey seasons are open, consider wearing some blaze orange so these hunters can see you. You can carry an inexpensive blaze-orange vest to wear as you walk to and from your stand.

Avoid wearing white or brown clothing. In dim light or darkness, use a flashlight. Some hunters affix childrens' flashing safety lights to their hats so they can be seen. If you encounter another hunter who doesn't see you, say hello or make a noise to attract attention.

Keeping safety in the forefront of your thinking can go a long way to avoiding an accident afield.

CHAPTER FOUR

Hunting Techniques

Hunters use dozens of techniques to outwit whitetails. Stand hunting, still-hunting and drives account for the vast majority of deer. But other methods—such as stalking, tracking, rattling, calling, using scents, using decoys—also have their devotees. Knowing how to hunt goes along with knowing where to hunt and when to hunt.

Stand Hunting

There is no official tally, but it seems reasonable to assume that more whitetails are killed by hunters in stands than by all other hunting methods combined. Taking a stand, or waiting in a likely spot for a deer to approach, is a very effective way to hunt. Hunting from a stand is best at times when deer are moving, such as early and late in the day, during the rut, or when other hunters are on the move.

Stand hunting works anywhere whitetails are found. It is a safe method for heavily hunted or populated areas because you are in one place and usually elevated above the ground. Hunting from a stand is the most consistent way for novice hunters to see deer. Many hunters spend the majority of their hunting time on stand. If you can sit—alert, silent and motionless—downwind from a deer trail or feeding area, sooner or later you'll see a deer.

Types of Stands

The term "deer stand" loosely defines places and objects used by hunters who are waiting for deer. A stand may be a stump on a northwoods ridge, a rusting farm implement beside a prairie wheat field, or an elevated shelter overlooking the brush country. Stands are divided into two categories: elevated stands and ground blinds. Either of them may be permanent or portable.

• The most common elevated stand is the tree stand, a platform typically placed 6 to 25 feet above the ground. Years ago, hunters believed deer did not look up, and even today whitetails are less likely to detect a hunter perched in a tree. However, hunters have learned that deer may indeed look up, especially older, more wary animals. Tree stand hunters generally use camouflage or screens to be inconspicuous.

Besides placing you above a deer's normal line of sight, an elevated stand offers other hunting advantages. Usually, you can see farther from an elevated position than from the ground, because you can look over and beyond any underbrush. From above the ground, human scent may disperse better and quicker, and not contaminate your hunting area. If a tree stand is comfortable and offers a good view of the surroundings, you can sit for longer periods of time—increasing your odds of seeing deer.

Permanent tree stands are built of lumber or natural materials in locations with consistent deer activity. A well-constructed permanent stand is safe and comfortable, and becomes part of the surroundings. Be sure you have landowner permission before building a permanent stand. Most public areas do not allow them.

Portable tree stands offer mobility. Many makes are available, falling into the categories of hang-on

Tree stand height is often dictated by the hunter's tolerance for being off the ground.

models, tree-crotch models, self-climbers and ladder stands. Freestanding tripod platforms are available, too. Choose a stand that is practical for where you hunt. Pay particular attention to platform size. A small platform may become uncomfortable if you intend to spend long hours in the tree. Weight and portability are other considerations, especially if you must walk a distance to reach your hunting location.

You can use a climbing stand to go up a bare tree trunk. Screw-in or strap-on steps are used with most portable stands. Place the steps so you come up the tree beside the platform. Remove the steps when you leave to lessen the chance that thieves will take your stand.

• Ground blinds can be simple or elaborate. Use them where elevated stands are impractical, unnecessary or unavailable. You can sit with your back against a tree trunk to disguise your outline or make a hiding place within a fallen tree. Use a few feet of camouflage material as a screen. Camouflaged tents with openings for shooting are commercially available. In open country, you can dig a shallow pit to use as a blind or hide behind hay bales.

When making a ground blind, be careful not to change natural features. Deer notice changes in their surroundings and are wary of them. A blind should be in place prior to your hunt so the deer become accustomed to it.

Permanent stands offer the most comfort, but require frequent maintenance to keep them safe. Deer become accustomed to such stands once they have weathered and the new-wood smell disappears.

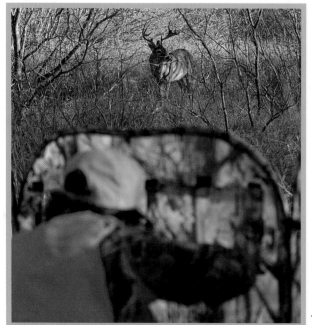

A good ground blind should be high enough to thoroughly conceal you while you're sitting on a stool.

Hang-on stands are also called fixed-position stands. These types are usually low priced due to their simplicity, and can be hung from just about any tree.

Self-climbing stands can be used only on trees with no branches below the desired stand height. They eliminate the need for tree steps or ladders, but are physically demanding to use.

Ladder stands are easy to climb; most are about 12 feet tall. For added safety attach the platform and ladder to the tree with straps or chains.

Tripod stands, up to 12 feet tall, are ideal in marshlands or brushlands without large trees. For best results, place them in the tallest cover available.

Crotch stands can be simply notched boards that are wedged tightly into a tree crotch, or manufactured with telescoping and hinged metal prongs on each end.

Stand Placement

Scout for trails, rutting activity and feeding areas to help you choose stand sites. Select locations near feeding fields, fencelines, forest openings, escape cover or anywhere you find abundant deer sign. Look for funnel locations where deer pass a certain place or trails leading to known bedding areas.

Pick a site that is inconspicuous, located in shadows, or screened with cover to break up your outline. Avoid having your human silhouette "skylighted" against an open background. Consider the prevailing wind direction and the angle of the sun when placing the stand. Always try to keep the wind in your face to control your scent and the sun at your back to avoid glare. If you put a stand on a ridge, morning air currents will carry your scent upward and away from the deer.

If possible, know the stand locations of other hunters who are in the vicinity, so you can avoid setting up your stand too close to another hunter. Generally, you should be at least twice the distance of your line of sight from other hunters. Don't place a stand along roads or trails regularly used by hunters or other people.

You can set up a stand anytime throughout the year, though most hunters do so during the weeks preceding the hunt. Select more than one stand site so you can move around to take advantage of changes in weather, hunting pressure and deer movements. If you are using portable stands, try to set them up at least a day prior to your hunt. In some situations, especially on heavily used public land, this may be impossible. Set up the stand so you can wait comfortably and have a full range of motion. Test the stand to make sure you can turn and shoot at deer approaching from various angles.

Judging Range

Place your stand close enough to a trail so deer pass within shooting range, but not so close that they detect your presence. Stands for bowhunting should be within 30 yards of where deer are likely to appear. You can shoot to greater distances with guns, though in most situations whitetails will be within 100 yards of your stand. In open country, distances may be greater.

According to surveys, more deer are taken by hunters on stand than by all other methods combined. The primary reason is obvious: A moving predator makes noise and is easily seen, while a motionless one makes no noise and is virtually invisible to whitetails. The following tips show you where to stand hunt throughout the season, regardless of whether you use elevated stands or ground stands.

- Always stay downwind or crosswind of the location where you expect to see deer. This lessens the chance that deer will smell you. If the wind changes during the day, move to another stand.
- Pick a spot that has enough cover to hide your silhouette and reduce glare from your face, glasses and hunting gear.
- Prune limbs and twigs from nearby trees and bushes to ensure a clear shot.
- Scrape away leaves from underfoot so you can move your feet silently when shifting position on the ground.

Benches

Forested ridges often have benches (sometimes called shelves, ledges or flats) that lie just below a ridge top. Benches are an important area to stand hunt regardless of whether you're pursuing deer in hilly farmland or true wilderness. Because benches are relatively flat, they are easy spots for deer to bed, feed and make scrapes. And, like saddles, benches are often used by deer in their daily travel routes. Prime stand locations (S) are shown above.

Edge Habitat

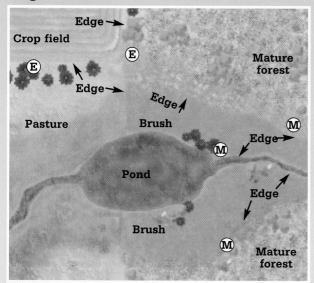

Quality deer habitat contains a large amount of edge – the zone between two different types of habitat, such as a forest and a field. An edge typically provides deer with a variety of foods and access to cover. Whenever you scout for a good stand location, look first along an edge. For evening hunts, place stands (E) on an edge and close to crop fields and other food sources; for midday and morning hunts, place stands (M) on an edge near thick bedding cover.

Primary Food Source

By glassing agricultural fields just before dark, you find that a number of deer are using an alfalfa field as their primary food source. A quick scouting trip on foot reveals that deer are bedding in thick brush near a lake. The main deer trail passes through the hardwoods between the wet slough and the open pasture. The best evening stands (E) are located close to the alfalfa field; the best morning stands (M) are closer to the bedding area.

Saddles

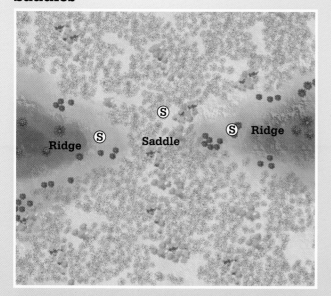

As whitetails travel through a forest, they usually walk the easiest route while taking advantage of available cover. For example, whitetails typically avoid climbing over steep ridges and simply pass between ridge tops in the saddle. Like funnels, saddles are excellent places to sit during the firearms deer opener. As hunters mill about the woods, deer travel through saddles en route to escape cover. Place stands (S) overlooking the saddle.

Funnels

Travel corridors, or funnels, are narrow bottlenecks formed where open fields, lakes, rivers or other obstacles force deer into a narrow area of cover. A funnel is one of the best places to be on a stand during the opening day of gun season. Hunting pressure typically keeps deer on the move throughout the day, and chances are excellent that many deer will be forced to travel through the funnel as they try to elude hunters. Place stands (S) overlooking the funnel.

Here are a few tips for making hunting from stands a little easier.

Screw-in steps help you climb any tree. Folding models take up less room in your pack, but cost more than nonfolding models (shown). If you plan to use the tree again, remove the steps and put matchsticks or twigs in the holes so you can easily find them next time.

Portable ladders are an alternative to screw-in steps. Most are made of aluminum and measure 12 to 14 feet in length. They break into 3- to 4-foot sections, strap securely to the tree and come with carrying straps for easy backpacking.

Reflective tacks or reflective adhesive strips applied to trees beforehand make it easy to find your stand in the dark. Before moving to a new stand, be sure to remove the tacks so you don't clutter the woods and confuse other hunters.

Use a range finder to accurately measure the distance to landmarks around your stand. Memorizing the distances will give you reference points when a deer appears.

Shooting Lanes

Removing a few saplings, a windfall or intervening branches makes it easier to see deer and get a clean shot. Clear twigs and brush that will interfere with your ability to move quietly or shoot. Use a pruning tool (where you have permission or the legal right) to cut shooting lanes radiating out from the stand. Unless you have the landowner's permission, do not cut down trees. Clear brush and fallen branches from your entrance/exit path to the stand, so you can approach quietly when you hunt there.

Take advantage of survey lines, logging skid trails and other lanes already cut in the forest. Deer often follow these lanes because they offer easy walking. You can also watch for crossing whitetails. Don't shoot down a lane unless you are certain no one is in your line of fire.

Hunting from a Stand

For stand hunters, patience is a virtue. Novices often find it is difficult to sit still for long periods of time. Wear enough clothes so you'll be warm and comfortable. In cold weather, carry extra clothes and put them on when you get to the stand, so you don't become overheated while walking. Bring snacks, a lunch and something to drink. Have a cushion to sit on.

When is the best time to go to a stand? In the morning, you want to be ready to hunt at the start of legal shooting time. This may mean walking to your stand in darkness. Have a well-marked route that you can follow with a flashlight. In late afternoon, go to your stand at least two hours before sunset to make the most of evening deer activity. Remember that you may see deer from a stand at any time of day. During gun season, it is a good idea to sit in your stand at noon when other hunters are leaving for lunch. They may push a deer past you.

Always walk upwind to reach a stand, so that your scent doesn't alert deer before you get there. Try not to walk through prime deer cover on your way to the stand. Don't cross fields or other openings that will allow the deer to see you from a distance. If you must go around a field, stay within the edge of the woods so you can't be seen. When you reach the stand, climb into it quietly. Don't make metallic, clinking noises that carry a long distance and are obviously human in origin. Prepare your gear in advance so you can settle in to hunt with a minimum of fidgeting.

Stay alert and watchful. Deer often seem to just materialize within your field of vision. A moment of inattention can mean a missed opportunity. Listen for footsteps, a breaking branch or other sounds. Watch not only where you expect the deer to appear, but all around you. Keep your movements to a minimum, slowly turning your head and searching with your eyes. Be silent.

When you see a deer, remain calm. Keep your actions slow and deliberate. Carefully, with a minimum of noise and motion, shift into a shooting position, preferably when the head of the deer is blocked from view by tree trunks or cover. Even a faint, unnatural sound, such as the metallic click of a gun safety, may alarm a deer. Pick a clear opening where you expect the deer to step out, and wait for it to do so. Carefully aim and shoot when you've confirmed that the deer is a legal animal.

After the shot, watch the deer. Even if it goes down, don't leave the stand. Sometimes a wounded animal may get up again. Gun hunters should wait at least a couple of minutes before going to the downed deer or following an animal that went beyond their field of vision. Bowhunters may wait an hour or more depending on the hit. Walk slowly and quietly in case you are approaching a wounded animal.

Changing Stand Locations

If you hunt from the same stand for several days or happen to spook a deer from the site, whitetails may shift their habits to stay away from your location. Use more than one stand to avoid "burning out" a site. Be careful not to disturb the area around your stand. Enter and exit quietly. If you have a hot spot, hunt there during weather conditions or at times of day when you are most likely to encounter deer.

Many hunters have favorite stands they use from year to year and consistently see deer. Often these stands are located along trails or habitat edges used by deer traveling from one place to another. During the rut, you are likely to see bucks using such trails. In Northern climates where deer migrate to wintering areas, different family groups of deer will use the same travelways from year to year. If you find one of these locations, by all means hunt it. But don't become so set in your ways that you refuse to try other stands.

You may decide to change stands during the course of a hunt if the wind changes direction or you think another location is better based on present conditions. Some hunters use a strategy where they sit for awhile and then move to another stand. If you happen upon a fresh scrape or other sign, sit down on a nearby stump and wait. The rutting buck may be close at hand.

TREE STAND SAFETY

Every year, hunters are seriously injured in tree stand accidents. Take these safety precautions whenever you use a tree stand:
- Always make sure the stand, ladder or climbing steps are secure before using them.
- Wear a safety harness whenever you are in a tree stand.
- Unload firearms or secure hunting arrows before climbing into a tree stand. You can use a rope to pull an unloaded gun or a bow into the tree.
- If you feel drowsy, climb down from the stand.
- Perform regular safety checks on all tree stands for deterioration or damage.
- Do not place stands in dead or diseased trees.
- Snow, ice or rain makes steps and platforms slippery. Use extra caution during inclement weather.
- Be sure that someone knows where your stands are located and when you'll be hunting from them.

Still-Hunting

Still-hunting sounds deceptively like a simple method, but it is really a very difficult way to kill a whitetail. The name for this hunting method is a misnomer, because the still-hunter actually sneaks through the woods, hoping to encounter a deer. To be successful, the hunter must avoid detection by sight, sound or scent. Still-hunting is typically a big-woods method because you need room to move around without encountering other hunters. However, you can sneak into any deer habitat under the right conditions.

Movement

Still-hunters use the wind to their advantage, always moving upwind or crosswind so the breeze doesn't deliver their scent to the deer. Weather conditions and terrain often cause shifts in wind direction, so you must always adjust your strategy to hunt into the wind. A stiff breeze is beneficial because it masks your sounds and movements. However, deer may be especially wary when winds are strong.

Unlike the stander, who waits for deer to come to a specific place or pass by along a trail, the still-hunter goes where deer are most likely to be. Slow

Sneaking silently is the key to successful still-hunting. Damp ground or fluffy snow quiets your footsteps; windy weather obscures any sounds you may make. Still-hunting is a good technique whenever hunting pressure is light.

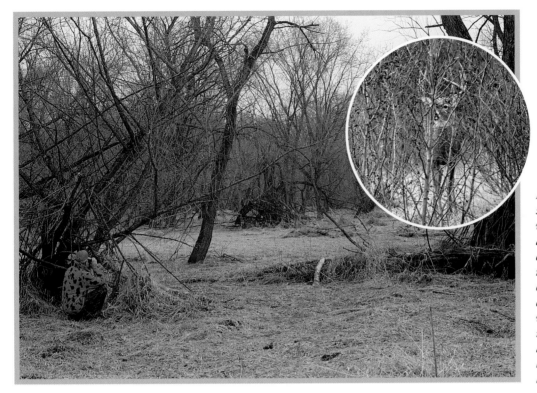

Because deer can easily spot your movement when still-hunting, take advantage of available cover, especially in more open areas. Stop often and scan the cover very carefully with binoculars. You may be able to pick out a deer that without binoculars would have been missed (inset).

and deliberate movements are necessary to approach whitetails. Take a step or two and then stand still, looking and listening for deer. Don't move again until you are certain no deer are nearby. Every step changes your view of the surroundings. Stop often.

Wet or snowy weather creates prime still-hunting conditions because you can move quietly in the woods. Take careful steps to avoid breaking sticks or making other sounds. Wear wool or similar soft clothing to minimize noise when you brush against vegetation. If possible, follow logging roads or pathways to walk quietly. Often, it is difficult to move without making sounds, but you should avoid the slow, steady footsteps that characterize a person walking.

Always use available cover to your advantage. Avoid unnecessary motions. Never step into openings; walk around the edge instead. Stand beside trees or behind brush and windfalls. Do not "skyline" yourself on hilltops. Sneak over the crest of ridges and carefully scrutinize new terrain before your body comes into full view.

Sight

The point of still-hunting is to get the drop on an unsuspecting whitetail. You must hear, see or even smell the deer first. Experienced still-hunters learn to look for a piece of a deer—an ear, a leg or the back line—that reveals an animal standing behind a screen of underbrush. Always look to the far edge of your field of vision because that is where a deer is most likely to be. If a whitetail detects your presence, but cannot catch your scent, it will often stand motionless until it can visually identify you as a human.

You should use binoculars to look for deer. Magnification makes it easier to spot deer screened by brush. While hunting, keep your scope magnification at 4X or less, so it will be easier to see a deer if you must make a quick shot.

Sound

If you hear a deer, stop and get ready. If possible, lean against a tree or use cover to break your outline. The animal may be very close when you actually see it. Use a grunt or doe call to attract deer that may not otherwise come in your direction. If hunting

Learning to still-hunt takes time—and patience. Hone your skills every chance you get. Soon you'll be seeing fewer "flags" and getting more shots.

Never "skyline" yourself by walking over a ridge in an upright position. Instead sneak or peek over the top and use whatever available trees or brush there is to hide your movement.

By yelping on a turkey call, you may be able to convince a deer that the sound of your movement came from a turkey. Use this tactic only when the turkey season is closed.

Monitor wind direction and rising and falling thermals by squeezing unscented powder from a bottle into the air. You may also toss some down or milkweed fluff in the air to test the wind.

conditions are quiet, you may be able to move and position yourself to intercept a deer that you can hear.

When still-hunting, you may hear a deer blow or make a sharp exhalation in alarm. The deer has heard or perhaps seen you, but hasn't identified you as a human. Very likely, it is just beyond your range of vision. Stop and scan the cover with your optics in the direction where you heard the deer. It probably won't approach any closer, but you may be able to pick it out in the brush. Respond to the deer with a couple of soft grunts. Often it will blow again and again before eventually walking off. Some hunters believe does are most likely to blow, but bucks do, too. You may be able to move closer by taking quick steps that sound like a walking deer. Getting a shot is difficult because the animal will bound off when it determines that you are not a deer.

When you spook a deer while still-hunting, it may bound a short distance and stop until it determines if you are following. Often, deer will walk away from an approaching still-hunter or simply move out of your line of travel. Deer do only what is necessary to avoid danger. Rarely will a deer run a long distance to get away from a lone hunter.

Options

Two hunters can still-hunt as a team. Agree upon a strategy before you begin hunting. Separate and move through the cover, staying 100 yards or more apart. Move slowly and pause frequently. One hunter may rattle or call. A pair of hunters is more likely to see a deer that investigates the sounds.

Opportunities to kill a deer when still-hunting often occur quickly and at close range. Unlike the stand hunter, who is hidden in ambush, a still-hunter usually has just a few seconds to shoot after a deer comes into view.

Once you identify your target, you must get into a shooting position without being seen or heard by the deer. Wait to move until the animal turns or steps behind cover. Keep your motions slow and minimal. Make no noise when clicking a safety or drawing an arrow. Take the first available clear shot at the vitals once you've determined that the deer is of legal size and/or sex. If you wait for the "perfect shot," the deer may become aware of your presence and get away.

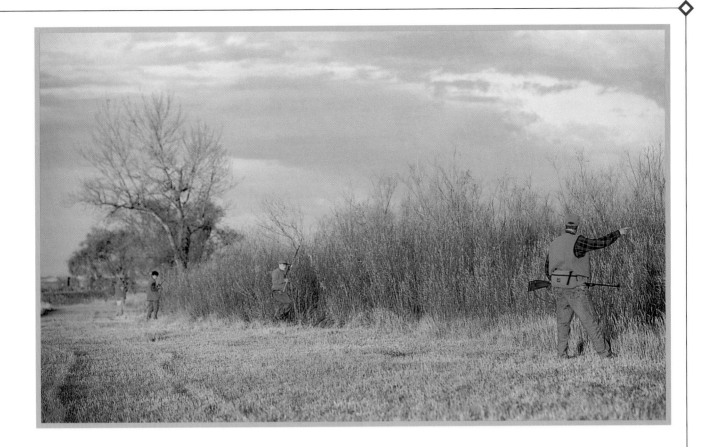

Driving

Deer drives are a team effort where a group of hunters are organized to walk through an area and push deer to other hunters posted on stands. An effective drive can be made by two hunters, or more than dozen. The key to success is knowing the whitetails' likely escape routes and placing standers to watch them. Driving is best used to roust deer from cover that is difficult to hunt by other methods.

Every deer drive begins with a plan and a leader to carry it out. When you are planning deer drives, a general rule of thumb is to not "bite off more than you can chew." The larger the area, the more likely whitetails will elude the hunters. Drives work best in patches of cover with definite boundaries—roads, field edges, creeks or fencelines. This makes it easier to determine where the deer are likely to be and helps keep the drive organized. For a deer drive to be effective and safe, every participant must understand his or her task and follow instructions.

You can make drives in all kinds of whitetail cover. Look for places the deer use as bedding areas or refuge. In the Northwoods, hunters make drives in conifer thickets or places where deer can be pushed to a forest trail or a clear-cut. Woodlots and cornfields are frequently driven in agricultural areas. Creek bottoms, set-aside fields and brushy draws are prime locations in open country. In the South, hunters sometimes use dogs to drive deer from thick cover.

The drive leader must consider several factors when planning a drive. What direction is the wind blowing? What escape routes are deer likely to use? How many standers are needed to cover those escape routes? Can they move into position without spooking the deer? Standers should be placed in locations where their scent will not be carried to deer fleeing ahead of the drivers.

The drive leader decides who walks and who posts. Generally, the most experienced hunters and best shots should take stands. Less experienced hunters can be drivers, provided they have a good sense of direction. Drives work best when the group has previously hunted together and most of the hunters are familiar with the land.

Making the Drive

Standers quietly move into their positions. Park vehicles away from the hunting area. Sneak along without talking. Whenever possible, place standers in elevated positions, such as in tree stands. This makes it easier to see deer and puts the line of fire toward the ground, which is safer. Standers must clearly understand where other standers are located and where the drivers will appear, and not take shots in those directions.

The drive leader arranges the drivers on the other side of the cover, keeping noise and commotion to a minimum. The distance between drivers is determined by the terrain and vegetation. In most situations, the drivers should be close enough to occasionally see one another as they make the drive. The drive leader can give each driver a compass bearing to help him or her stay on course. In some hunting parties, drivers are unarmed. If the drivers carry firearms, firm rules should be established to ensure only safe shots are taken.

A signal from the drive leader begins the drive. The drivers should move forward at an agreed-upon pace, typically a slow walk. Making excessive noise is unnecessary because the deer will sense the presence of drivers and move ahead of them. It is more important that drivers go through heavy cover where deer may try to hide and let them pass by. Watch for whitetails that try to double back and sneak between the drivers or cut out from the flanks.

You don't need a gang of hunters to make a drive. Often, two or three hunters working in concert are more effective. Small drives are most often a combination of stand and still-hunting. While one hunter waits in an elevated stand or ground blind, the other hunter sneaks through likely cover and tries to push a deer toward the stander. This is an excellent midmorning tactic because both hunters can sit during the prime early hours and then one can make a push to the other.

Two or three hunters can also move deer from small islands of cover in agricultural areas. Whitetails, especially bucks, will hide in a weedy patch, a fencerow or a cattail slough where most hunters are unlikely to look for them. Try to stealthily approach small covers from opposite directions. Expect fast shots at running deer.

With snow, sometimes you'll happen upon fresh deer tracks and be able to predict where the whitetail is likely to go. One hunter follows the tracks while one or two other hunters, circle around and post in likely locations. The tracker must be patient and give the standers sufficient time to get into position before going after the deer.

DRIVING SAFETY

Drives inherently have more safety risks than other hunting methods because the deer may go between hunters. It is imperative that every hunter participating in a drive puts safety first. To prevent accidents, consider the following:

- Always follow the drive leader's instructions.
- Never shoot in the direction of other hunters, even if they are out of sight.
- When walking, don't get ahead of the other hunters on the drive.
- When taking a stand, consider the directions where you can safely shoot. When you see a deer, make sure it is within one of your safe shooting windows before pulling the trigger.
- Only shoot at deer running across open fields if you have a safe backstop.
- If you are uncomfortable with the safety skills of another hunter in the party, quietly voice your concerns to the drive leader.
- Be aware that other hunters who are not members of your party may be in the drive area.

Hunters with knowledge of whitetail behavior can successfully drive the animals toward waiting standers posted strategically along excape routes.

Different terrains require different methods. Here are some tried-and-true setups that are sure to increase your odds.

"Funnel drives" take advantage of funnels through which deer are forced by drivers (D). Funnel drives require fewer standers (S) than drives through wider expanses of cover. To prevent deer from slipping back through drivers in heavy cover, a middle driver (M) drops out and takes a stand as the drive passes the narrowest area and continues.

"Ravine drives" also work well with two hunters, but wide ravines require more drivers. Select a ravine where the wind is blowing parallel to it and toward its head. Hunter A starts at the bottom of the ravine and begins walking uphill. Hunter B is on stand near the head, but about 75 yards in from the tip, for shots at slow-moving deer.

"Hopscotch drives" are ideal for two hunters. They begin the drive from opposite ends of the cover. Hunter A moves slowly toward hunter B for about half an hour; A then sits quietly for about half an hour as B closes the gap. Because each hunter alternates between driving and posting, both have an equal chance of seeing deer.

Stalking

Hunting an animal you've sighted is called stalking and is an exceptionally challenging way to kill a deer. While in some instances, particularly in the West, you may stalk deer while hunting with a gun, most often the technique is used by experienced bowhunters. To sneak within archery range of a whitetail is among hunting's greatest accomplishments.

A stalk begins by spotting a deer that is out of range. Find a concealed vantage point where you can look across the terrain with a spotting scope or binoculars. You may see deer feeding in fields or clear-cuts. Scan sunny ridges for bedded whitetails. When you see a deer, then look for a landmark so you can get a fix on its position. Be sure to pick a landmark that will be visible as you move closer and from different angles.

Stalking begins with glassing the terrain to find the best route. Avoid crossing any openings such as (1) a cornfield in the bottom of the valley, and take advantage of (2) logging roads or deer trails to move as quietly as possible. As you walk, watch for other deer. If another one detects you, it may snort or flag, warning the deer you're stalking.

Plan your stalk to approach from downwind. Even if your vantage point is a long way from the deer, stay out of sight as you move into position to begin the stalk. Go as quickly as you can.

Wet or snowy conditions are best for stalking because you'll make the least amount of noise. Stay out of sight as long as possible. Crouch like a cat stalking a songbird in your backyard. The closer you get to the deer, the more difficult the stalk becomes. Never move when the animal is alert and studying its surroundings, even if it isn't looking at you. Avert your eyes if the deer is looking in your direction. You don't want to make eye contact. If the deer is feeding or walking, it may be easier to sneak to a position where the deer will come closer to you.

Sometimes, the deer will hear you make a noise or somehow sense your presence. It may look your way, perhaps even staring to try to discern what you are. If it can't smell you or detect movement, it may eventually look away and show little concern. Be aware, though, that deer quickly notice something out of the ordinary. Even if you are camouflaged, a whitetail may identify you as an object it hasn't seen before. If it does, you'll have a tough time getting any closer to it.

Stalking in Standing Corn

A version of the stalk is to sneak from row to row through a standing cornfield. Whitetails frequently use corn as secure feeding and bedding areas. From a downwind or crosswind position, sneak through the field perpendicular to the rows. The sound of a breeze rustling the stalks will help conceal any noise you make. Look down a row before you step into it.

Taking the Shot

Deer killed by stalking are often taken at close range, especially if you are bowhunting. Slow movements and patience have put you in a shooting position. Now you must move even slower. If at all possible, wait until the deer's head is behind a tree or some other object before lifting your gun or drawing your bow. Otherwise, make your movements so slow that they are imperceptible. It may take minutes to get into a shooting position.

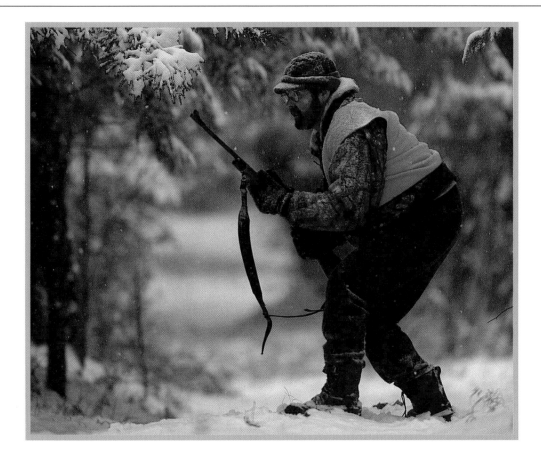

Tracking

The ability to follow deer tracks in a variety of conditions is the mark of a good hunter. Tracking skills are essential to following a deer after you make a shot. A print in the soil, a turned-over leaf or a broken twig may be your clues to finding a mortally wounded deer. Such tracking skills are acquired only through experience.

Another set of skills is needed to track deer as part of your hunting strategy, a method typically used when snow blankets the ground. You must be able to recognize fresh deer tracks, have a general idea where the animal is head-ed, and then follow them quickly and quietly so you can close the dis-tance for a shot. Hunters often track deer in

Tracking deer in snow demands concentration and patience (top). New tracks in snow (above) or soil (right) have distinctive characteristics.

North Country areas with a low deer density, where stand hunting is unproductive.

About Tracks

Generally, fresh deer tracks have well-defined edges. With very fresh tracks, you may find muddy water where the deer walked through a puddle or even see water oozing into muddy tracks. Older tracks have crumbling edges and are hard to the touch. In snow, fresh tracks will be soft when you touch them. Old tracks have frozen edges.

Tracking Strategy

The best tracking conditions are soft, fresh snow, because you can follow tracks with less likelihood of becoming confused by the tracks of other deer, especially on well-trodden trails. Fresh snow is quiet underfoot, so you can walk without making noise. Often deer are on the move during and after snowfalls.

Tracking is rarely a matter of finding tracks and following them until you catch up with the deer. Most of the time, the deer will become aware of your presence before you see it and bound away. If the animal beds, it will be watching its backtrail. Also, deer have a tendency to go through thickets and tangles that most hunters would rather avoid. If you try to stay on the tracks, most likely you'll make noise in the heavy cover.

A better strategy is to think like a deer. Follow the tracks far enough to get a sense of where the deer is headed. Pay keen attention to wind direction because the deer will walk upwind or crosswind. Then plan your course. Perhaps you can walk parallel to the tracks and watch for the deer out ahead. In hilly terrain, you may find a vista where you can watch for the deer crossing a ridge or valley. Often, the best strategy is to guess where the deer is going and then try to intercept it.

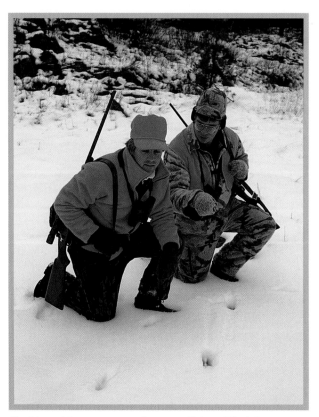

Tracking with a partner can be more efficient, if both hunters communicate clearly and don't walk over the track, which would ruin any chance for learning about the deer and its direction.

Tracking with a Partner

Two hunters can track better than one. Working as a team, one hunter closely follows the tracks, while the other still-hunts on a parallel course. By staying slightly ahead of the tracker, the still-hunter may be able to get into a position for a shot.

Sometimes, in a variety of conditions, you may encounter very fresh deer tracks. Immediately begin to hunt as if the deer is close at hand. Often, it is. Stand still, watch and listen. If you know the country, you may be able to head off the deer. Hustle (quietly) to your ambush point and wait. If the deer doesn't appear, still-hunt toward the place where you first saw its tracks.

Go for Bucks

Tracking is a good way to hunt bucks, especially when they are active during the rut. It is easy to recognize their large, solitary tracks. Generally, bucks appear to be going someplace, headed on a straight course. Does are more likely to meander. A good strategy is to cut away from the tracks and try to beat the buck to his destination.

If you follow a buck, it will likely lead you to other deer. A rutting buck will be looking for does or it may associate with local family groups. Tracking gets tricky when you run into other deer because it may be hard to follow the original set of tracks. Also, you are more likely to startle a deer, which may alarm others.

Tracks and strides (right) may give clue to the sex of the deer. Tracks of mature bucks can be nearly as wide as they are long and have rounded tips. Doe and yearling buck hooves are narrower and have more sharply pointed tips. In rocky terrain, however, any older deer can have worn hooves with rounded tips.

Mature bucks place their back hoof to the rear of the front hoof; does usually place their rear hoof on top of the front track.

Mature bucks have an average of 6 inches between left and right tracks; a doe's track averages 2 inches wide.

Mature bucks have an average stride of 20 inches; a doe's stride is only 14 inches.

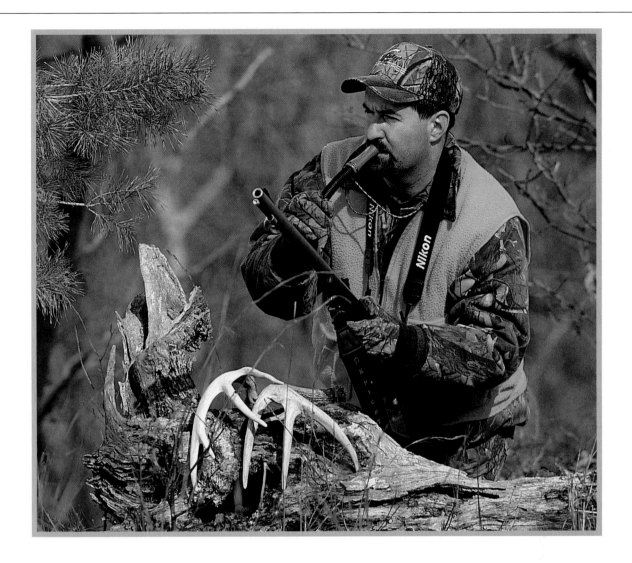

Rattling, Calling and Using Scents

Whitetails can be attracted to sounds they expect to be made by other deer. The clatter of antlers, guttural grunts of a rutting buck, and distress bleats are sounds you can make to draw deer out of the cover. Though effective, noise-making strategies require confidence because they seem counter to the silent approach that typifies whitetail hunting.

Various scents are used to attract deer, too. A whitetail uses its keen nose not only to detect danger, but to find food and other deer. A variety of commercial and natural scents can be used to lure deer or to cover up your human scent.

Rattling

Before, during and after the rut, you can mimic the sounds of fighting whitetails to attract bucks. Rattling is a hunting technique that originated in Texas, but is used successfully wherever whitetails are found. It is one of the best ways to overcome the innate wariness of an adult buck and make it come to you. Veteran deer hunters consider rattling one of the most exciting hunting methods. However, rattling is generally inefficient during firearms seasons in areas with heavy hunting pressure.

To rattle, all you need is a pair of antlers not attached to the skull plate. You can use shed antlers or saw the antlers from an intact rack. Each antler should have three or four tines. Saw off the brow tines to make it easier to hold the antlers. If you don't have real deer antlers, commercial substitutes are available, including synthetic antlers and various rattling bags or calls. Some commercial products are more convenient to carry in the field than the real thing.

Here are a few good rattling strategies:

• Quietly approach your rattling site, taking care not to spook the deer with human sounds or scent. Remember, the deer must be within earshot of your location to be attracted to the sound. You can set up in a ground blind or tree stand, so long as you have a good view—especially downwind. Two hunters can take separate positions.

• You can use a cover scent to disguise your scent and place an attractor scent downwind and to the side of your location. However, the more you move around, the more likely you are to alert whitetails to your presence. Make sure your gun or bow is positioned so you can pick it up with minimal movement. A buck may appear at any time once you begin rattling.

• Start out by clicking the tines gently a few times, then pause for a few minutes. Rattle more loudly the second time. Make it sound as though two bucks are clashing and then stepping back. Keep your rattling time short—a couple of minutes is about right. Pause for several minutes and then rattle again. The entire sequence should take 15 or 20 minutes. When you are done, wait patiently for approaching deer because a big buck may take his time.

• You can add realism to your rattling by incorporating other sounds. Start your sequence with a few soft grunts. Rake the antlers in the brush or leaf litter. Break sticks or stamp your feet to make the sounds of a fight.

Calling

Sounds imitating whitetail vocalizations can be used to attract deer. An array of calls are commercially available. Get a tape or video to learn how to properly use calls because you'll likely have few opportunities to actually hear deer making these sounds. Calling is effective throughout the whitetail range, but is best used in conjunction with other hunting strategies.

• The most commonly used call is the grunt made by rutting bucks, either when alone or accompanying a doe. Bucks are attracted to grunts because they expect a doe to be in the vicinity. When using a commercial call, take care not to blow too loudly. Start with soft grunts and increase volume as necessary. Blow a short series of grunts and then wait. Use the call sparingly and when you think a buck is nearby.

• A fawn separated from its mother will bleat. You can use a bleat call to attract a doe or, occasionally, a buck. Bleat three or four times, spaced a few seconds apart.

• Sometimes you can make a deer pause or look in your direction by whistling. Some hunters have the blows, snorts and wheezes that are part of whitetail alarm and breeding vocalizations in their calling repertoire. However, these calls are on the periphery of hunting strategies.

Among the many styles of call available on the market today are the BucGrunter Deer Call (1), Adult Doe Estrus Bleat (2) and Young Doe Estrus Bleat (3) from Hunters Specialties; and the Rubberneck Call from Primos (4).

Using Scents

Deer can be lured into range using scents. White-tails have powerful olfactory senses that allow them to communicate, find food and avoid preda-tors. Deer usually walk upwind or crosswind so they can use their nose to determine what lies ahead. Hunters take advantage of this trait when they employ scent strategies.

Hunters typically use deer urine, scents derived from whitetail glands, food attractors or scents intended to cover human odor. Dozens of com-mercial scent products are available. Some hunters use glands taken from deer.

• Whitetail urine is commonly used as an attractor. Doe-in-estrus urine is used to attract bucks. You can apply the scent to your boots as you walk to your stand, place urine-soaked rags or cottonballs in locations that will draw deer to your stand, or make a mock scrape and use a drip dispenser to slowly release urine. When setting up attractor scent stations, be careful to place them so the deer won't smell you as they approach.

• Whitetails communicate with scent glands located at various points on their body. Commercial scents derived from these secretions can be used when making a mock scrape or at other scent stations. Some hunters cut the tarsal gland, located on the inside of the lower hind leg, from a freshly killed buck. You can rub the tarsal scent on your boots or use it at a scent station. Rags or boot pads soaked with gland scents and urine can be used to lay down a scent trail leading to your stand.

• Scents smelling like apples, acorns, persimmons or other deer foods are used to lure deer. While deer will investigate these smells, they are unlikely to travel any distance to do so. You can place food scents near your stand to distract deer or get them to pause for a shot.

• Bowhunters in particular go to great lengths to mask their human odors because they must get very close to whitetails in order to get a shot. Strong nat-ural cover scents, such as skunk musk and fox urine were once popular. Some hunters rub their clothing with freshly crushed pine or cedar branches. Re-member, the best way to keep a deer from smelling you is to use the wind to your advantage.

• Dedicated trophy hunters use a scent-control sys-tem that utilizes deodorizing chemicals combined with special odor-containment clothing to elimi-nate human scent. Soda-based and oxidizing liq-uids and powders are available that will neutralize human smells, which are produced by bacteria, body oils and perspiration. With meticulous atten-tion to detail, you can control human scent enough so that a deer approaching from down-wind will be less likely to detect you.

All clothing should be washed with scent-free detergents and stored outdoors or in scent-free containers. On the day of the hunt, you should wash with scent-free soap and shampoo. The neu-tralizing chemicals are applied to your body, all clothing and hunting gear prior to the hunt. A scent-containment suit is worn under your outer layer of clothing. Special coveralls are worn over your hunting clothes while traveling to the hunt-ing area to avoid scent contamination. Wear rub-ber boots (leather holds scents) and walk slowly to your hunting site to prevent scent-producing per-spiration. Proper preparation will allow you to remain scent-free during the hunt.

Scents include gland scents from Hunters Specialties (far left), masking scents such as fox or skunk from Tink's (left) and attracting scents from Browning (above).

Using Decoys

The use of deer decoys is a relatively new advancement in deer hunting. Whitetails can be drawn to a dummy deer, especially when combined with rattling, calling or the use of scent. For safety reasons, decoying is primarily a bowhunting strategy. Don't use decoys when gun seasons are open or in places where you are likely to run into other hunters. When carrying a decoy, be sure you are wearing at least a blaze-orange hat. Tie some orange material to the decoy or carry it in an orange bag.

Full-body and silhouette decoys are available. The advantage of using a decoy is that it gives an approaching deer a visual focus, which means it is less likely to see you hiding nearby. You can buy both doe and buck decoys, which may attract deer for different reasons. A buck initially lured by rattling may approach with less caution when it sees a decoy in the place where it expects sparring bucks to be. Deer are social animals and will approach a doe decoy out of curiosity. In a feeding field, a deer may feel more secure if it can be near another whitetail—or a decoy.

Here are a few good decoy strategies:

• Decoys are often used in situations where deer can see them from a distance, such as fields or forest openings. They are most effective when used early or late in the day, when deer are more likely to be on the move. Set up before daylight for early-morning

hunts or in the afternoon for evening hunts. The trick is to place the decoy without being seen by the deer.

• Use a scent blocker to rid the decoy of human smells and attractor scents to lure deer. Position yourself downwind of the decoy, taking care to ensure a whitetail won't smell you as it approaches. If you rattle or call, stop when you spot a deer coming in. Otherwise, the whitetail may pinpoint you as the source of the sound.

• During the rut, set up a decoy near scrapes or where buck activity is evident. Use doe-in-estrus or gland-based scents that will attract a buck in rut. A buck in full rut may approach the decoy quickly and physically interact with it—trying to mate or fight with it. To fool especially wary old bucks, you may find success using more than one decoy, such as a buck and a doe.

• Look for ways to add movement to your decoy setup. Some hunters tie a white cloth to the tail so it flickers in the breeze. You can tie a fishing line to the cloth and pull to make it move in calm conditions.

• Depending on the situation, a deer may walk right into a decoy or circle cautiously. Don't expect the decoy to be foolproof. The longer a whitetail watches it, the more likely it will decide the motionless dummy is a fake. However, a deer preoccupied with the decoy may come close enough to you to present an opportunity for a shot.

Decoys come in three basic types, most of which have removable antlers and can be converted from a buck to a doe: three-dimensional, lightweight plastic foam decoys (left); two-dimensional hinged decoys (center); and full-body hard plastic decoys (right).

According to Toby Bridges, a dedicated muzzleloader and trophy whitetail hunter, "The key to tagging a certified trophy buck, one of those heavy, old bruisers with the rocking-chair rack everybody dreams of, is to hunt where one lives." He adds, "That sounds obvious, but it's the ultimate reality of trophy hunting. You can have the best equipment and the best tactics in the world. You can have the sharpest eyes and be the best stalker since Daniel Boone. But if there aren't any old bucks living where you hunt, the only thing you'll get is disappointment."

Toby is right, of course. The most important part of any trophy whitetail hunt is finding an area where bucks have survived long enough to grow large antlers. Trophy bucks are almost always old bucks.

Preparation Basics

Hunting for large, mature bucks is most successful in areas with light hunting pressure, low to moderate deer densities and buck-to-doe ratios of 1:2 or 1:3. Wildlife management agencies can provide you with these statistics. Don't be concerned if hunter-success statistics are low. High hunter success generally means only that large numbers of immature bucks are being taken each year.

As a rule, areas with high deer densities are hunted so heavily that bucks rarely live past 3½ years. In some places, 90 percent of all antlered bucks are killed each season. And if there is a high ratio of females to bucks, the males don't engage in normal, competitive rutting behavior and are therefore difficult to lure with rattling, calling, decoying or scrape-hunting strategies.

Here are a few things you can do to up your odds of learning where the big bucks live:

• Study topographical maps and aerial photos to find isolated habitat where few hunters penetrate.

• Talk to rural mail carriers, UPS drivers and farmers who may have seen large bucks.

• If possible, scour the winter range after snow melt, looking for shed antlers.

• Drive area roads at dawn and dusk, and watch feed fields with binoculars.

• Visit local taxidermists and learn what the trophy potential is for the area. What's the usual rack size? How many record-book bucks are taken each year?

When you've discovered a suitable hunting area, begin narrowing your search. Your goal is to locate at least three trophy bucks so you'll have hunting opportunities throughout the season, even if someone else kills one of "your"

bucks. If you actually spot the bucks, great; but it's likely you'll have to settle for second-hand evidence, such as finding large tracks or big shed antlers, or a description from an eyewitness. Try to get permission to hunt as much land as possible. Your chances of harvesting a buck will be greatest if you have permission to hunt the land around his bedding area, because this is where he spends most of his time.

How to Hunt for Trophies

Once you've confirmed the existence of a mature buck, the hard part is over and the fun begins. Forget the old myths about superbucks. There is nothing supernatural about a trophy buck, and no reason for you to feel intimidated. A stupendous set of antlers simply means the buck is old, and the main reason he's old is probably because hunting pressure has been light in his territory. The argument about whether an old buck is more intelligent than other deer will probably never be resolved, but one thing is certain: During the rut your buck will be susceptible to the same strategies that work with younger bucks— rattling, decoying, calling and using scents.

But there's no denying that the trophy buck is a special animal that requires a special hunter with unusual dedication, patience and restraint. For one thing, a mature trophy buck is calmer and less energetic than the young guys. Rather than dashing about and exposing himself to hunters, he's learned to lay low and watch carefully, knowing that most humans will overlook him. As a veteran of many seasons, he's used to seeing, smelling and hearing hunters at dawn and dusk, so he generally waits until night to move about.

The old buck is a creature of leisure and habit, with periodic moments of energy. He lies resting most of the daylight hours, and often chooses the shortest distances possible between food, water and bed. If he found refuge on an island during one hunting season, he'll remember to seek out the same island in following seasons. Only during the rut does the old boy rouse himself for frenzied action—this is your best chance for taking him.

Seasoned trophy hunters know that information is power. Learn as much as possible about your quarry: Where, when and what does your buck eat? Where does he drink? Where does he sleep, walk, rub, scrape and chase females? Where does he hide when hunting pressure gets intense? It may take several years to piece together such a profile, but once you know your buck this well, you're ready for the most memorable hunt of your life.

CHAPTER FIVE

Regional Differences

The white-tailed deer has such a wide range in North America that you can hunt it in ecosystems ranging from boreal forests to subtropical jungles to western deserts. While the habits of deer remain largely the same, hunting tactics vary with the habitat, climate and local customs. Traveling deer hunters find these regional differences add to the challenge and charm of the hunt.

State and provincial hunting seasons and regulations vary, too. Generally, they are based on the science of deer population management, safety considerations and social traditions. Land access and ownership affect the hunt as well. Some places have large tracts of public hunting land, while in others hunting access is controlled by private landowners. Leasing land for hunting has become prevalent in recent years as deer hunting has become increasingly popular. It is difficult to find places where a knock on the landowner's door and a handshake will gain you permission to hunt.

In many areas, you can seek the services of a deer hunting guide or outfitter. For a price, you will get a place to hunt, likely with pre-placed stands. Some outfitters have access to extensive property and specialize in trophy bucks. A hunt with a trophy outfitter in Canada or Texas is a dream trip for many hunters.

The Heartland

Most North American deer hunting occurs in the eastern half of the continent, in habitat that is a mix of hardwood forest and agricultural fields.

This type of cover is found from the Eastern Seaboard to the Midwest and represents the heartland of whitetail hunting. Deer populations are abundant across this landscape, and most states allow hunters to kill more than one deer, usually through a permit system. Some heartland states, particularly in the Midwest, have the combination of limited hunting access, fertile soils and good genetics that make them consistent producers of record-book bucks. Most heartland deer can feed in farm crops, although in hilly or mountainous regions they may rely on mast crops such as acorns.

Wildlife management areas and publicly owned forests are scattered throughout the heartland. Public areas are usually heavily hunted, but with careful scouting you can have a successful hunt. Many heartland hunters prefer to hunt on private land. Due to deer hunting's popularity, it is necessary to secure landowner permission to hunt long before the season begins. Many properties are hunted year after year by the family and friends of the landowner. Leasing of private lands for hunting is increasingly common, especially in areas that produce trophy bucks.

Firearms seasons attract the greatest numbers of hunters and account for most of the annual deer harvest. The firearms season is an unofficial holiday in some rural locales, with large numbers of hunters taking time off from work or school to go hunting. In many agricultural areas within the heartland, firearms hunters are restricted to using shotguns with slugs. To beat the crowds, many

Bagging a buck is a sign of success, no matter which area of North America you hunt.

Bowhunters get a head start on firearms hunters in the heartland where competition for hunting land can be quite intense.

heartland hunters take up bowhunting, which gives them longer hunting seasons and better opportunities to get permission to hunt on private property. Late-season muzzleloader hunts continue to gain fans, especially among hunters seeking less hunting pressure and a challenging hunt.

Stand hunting is the preferred heartland hunting tactic, because hunters generally have limited land access or, especially during firearms hunting seasons, must contend with heavy hunting pressure. Heartland bowhunters employ all the modern tactics and have been pioneers in the use of scents, calls and decoys. The archers take advantage of increased whitetail activity during the pre-rut and rut periods, which in some heartland states occur prior to the start of gun seasons. Late-season hunters often key-in on food sources, such as unharvested crops or crop residues.

The Northwoods

The northern forests of the Upper Great Lakes, the Northeast, and eastern Canada have deep-rooted deer hunting traditions. Whitetails proliferated in the Northwoods a century ago when logging activity and large fires created an abundance of young forest habitat. This is big country, typified by large expanses of unbroken forest and minimal agricultural activity. In winter, Northwoods deer migrate to yarding areas, usually cedar swamps or similar coniferous cover, where they find shelter from cold temperatures and deep snows. Mortality caused by severe winter weather can decimate a Northwoods deer population.

Low deer population densities make Northwoods hunting challenging. Hunters often set up stands along deer trails or near forest openings, such as recently logged areas, where there is an abundance of browse and other natural foods. Still-hunting and tracking are effective, especially when there is snow on the ground. Firearms hunting is the traditional method, with seasons generally occurring during the rut. October archery hunting is excellent.

Most Northwoods hunting occurs on public land or large private tracts, such as paper company holdings. Many hunters have deer camps where they gather annually with family and friends during the firearms deer season. The social traditions associated with a Northwoods deer camp are often as important to the hunters as the hunt itself. Hunting pressure can range from minimal in remote areas to heavy in more settled regions. Across most of the North, enough bucks elude hunters and survive the winters to reach trophy sizes.

Northern hunting areas are especially challenging when the weather turns toward winter. But it also can be the most rewarding experience.

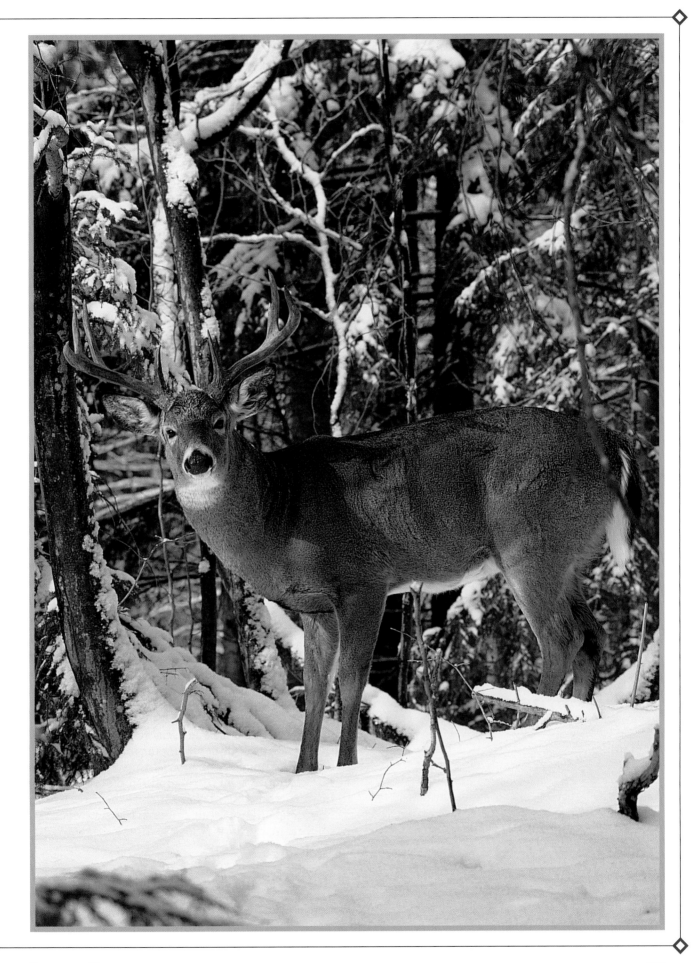

The Suburbs

Whitetail hunters who live in metropolitan areas don't need to travel far to find good hunting. Suburban deer populations have exploded throughout the whitetail range. Parks, undeveloped properties, stream corridors, and even residential neighborhoods create habitat conditions suitable for whitetails.

Local ordinances often prohibit or restrict hunting, so deer numbers grow unchecked. Human perceptions of suburban whitetails go from novelty to nuisance when vehicle collisions, damage to shrubs and gardens, and the threat of Lyme disease escalate. In such situations, hunting is a practical means to control the deer population.

Special hunts or seasons, often with liberal antlerless deer limits, are used by game managers to reduce suburban whitetail numbers. Bowhunting is the preferred management method because it is quiet and unobtrusive.

In densely populated areas, hunters may be restricted to public parks or similar green spaces, which are closed to other uses during the hunt. If the municipality contains a fair amount of undeveloped land, hunters may be allowed to access properties where they have permission to hunt. In some metropolitan areas, responsible local bowhunters have formed organizations that specialize in suburban hunts.

Often in the suburbs, hunters are confined to small woodlots or vacant lands in the midst of development. The sounds of traffic, children playing and other human activity form the backdrop for the hunt. Stand hunting is the safest, most practical tactic for suburban deer. A good suburban hunter is mostly unnoticed and makes minimal disruptions for the people who live nearby.

Precise shot placement and prompt recovery of downed animals is of utmost importance. Harvested deer should be moved discreetly from the hunting area. Suburban hunting has unique challenges, but offers many hunters the opportunity to hunt close to home.

Hunting near a residential area comes with additional challenges. Not only must you be quiet to not spook a deer, you must be careful not to draw the attention of nonhunting people in the area. It's imperative that the kill be clean, and the deer is found and removed quickly.

As suburbs have crept into the countryside and more and more people have built homes in the heart of deer habitat, whitetails have adapted to city life. In fact, urban deer populations may contain more big bucks than herds in more traditional deer habitat. Large homes built on several acres are often closed to hunting. Deer thrive in these situations as long as there is cover, some browse and good bedding sites. With little or no hunting, good food and cover, bucks grow to older ages and trophy size.

In many of these areas, whitetail populations get out of hand. Residents who started out with an affection for the brown-eyed doe in the back-yard often change their minds when hoards of deer eat every shrub, flower and vegetable on their property. Whitetails are hosts to Lyme disease, a serious human ailment, and collisions between deer and autos are costly and potentially dangerous. More and more communities are facing the problem of too many deer.

One solution to the urban deer problem is to allow bowhunting in town. Bowhunting poses few hazards to hunters or nearby nonhunters; it's quiet and unobtrusive, and it can control a deer population.

Of course, getting permission to hunt is important for any deer hunter, but it's absolutely critical for the urban hunter. In many eastern communities with urban deer problems, groups of experienced, ethical bowhunters have formed informal clubs that landowners and home owners can contact when they want deer removed.

These clubs have membership qualifications and ethics rules that are strictly enforced. Members must meet with landowners and become acquainted with their concerns.

Once a bowhunter has permission to hunt in a suburb, he (or she) should make an extraordinary effort to keep landowners in the area happy. If he arrives before daylight, he should avoid making noise that might disturb the residents. He should do his best to maintain a friendly one-to-one relationship with people in the neighborhood. A little courtesy helps keep the backyards open for hunting the next fall.

Municipalities initiate controlled bowhunts to reduce deer numbers, That means harvesting female deer is critical. While most hunters want to kill bucks, they will do more to control the herd by taking does. Once the meat gets to the table, nobody will know the difference. Of course, when that once-in-a-lifetime trophy walks into range, there's generally time to make an exception.

A bowhunter in the suburbs can better his or her chances by hunting strips of timber (the thicker the cover, the better) used as travel corridors by deer. Heavily used trails, lines of tree rubs and scrapes during the fall rut mark these corridors. A hunter using a stand should get settled well before daylight to avoid disturbing deer moving through the corridors to their bedding sites in early morning. It's smart to approach the stand from a different direction each day to disperse human scent and prevent deer from identifying a pattern of human use.

Central Canadian Prairies

The prairies and transitional forests of Manitoba, Saskatchewan and Alberta have produced some of the largest white-tailed bucks on the continent, including the present world-record typical, killed in 1993 by local farmer Milo Hansen in Biggar, Saskatchewan.

For many U.S. hunters, a Canadian whitetail hunt is a dream trip. Numerous hunting outfitters exist to fulfill that dream. Hunting occurs on prairie farms, as well as in the northern forest, where bait piles are sometimes used to attract deer. Biting cold and snow are normal hunting conditions. Nevertheless, the opportunity to kill the buck of a lifetime lures thousands of American hunters north of the border every year.

Hunting in the wide-open spaces of the Central Canadian Prairies is a two-edged sword. It means being able to see the deer from a long way, but it means the deer can see you, too.

The West

Whitetails thrive on the open prairie and plains west of the Mississippi River, as well as in mountain and desert regions. Western whitetails are not widely distributed across the western landscape, but are mostly found in association with row crop agriculture, stream corridors or dense woody cover. They are often abundant in good habitat, although western deer are susceptible to occasional die-offs from severe weather or diseases such as EHD (epizootic hemorrhagic disease). Whitetail hunting, particularly for trophy bucks, has become more popular in the West, but often they receive less attention from hunters than other big-game species.

Most western whitetail hunting occurs on private lands, although good public hunting opportunities are available. In situations where whitetails are abundant and lightly hunted, you may easily gain permission to hunt private farms and ranches. In many regions, ranchers charge an access fee. In top trophy areas, the best ranches are leased or controlled by hunting outfitters. An outfitted hunt with a reputable guide is the surest way to kill a trophy western whitetail.

Western whitetails typically spend their time in the heaviest cover available, where they can be hunted at close range by archers or black powder hunters using traditional tactics. Rifle hunters often place stands near feeding fields early and late in the day, where shots of 100 to 300 yards are not uncommon. During the day, they still-hunt or stalk in breaks and bottoms the deer use as refuge and bedding areas.

Brush Country

The brush country of South Texas and northern Mexico has long been a popular deer hunting destination. Although the bucks are small in stature, mature animals often sport trophy-size antlers. The best hunting occurs on private ranches, which charge hefty fees for hunting access. Some large ranches are surrounded by high fences to contain the deer.

Brush-country hunters often use platform towers to see over the dense brush. They use rifles chambered for long-range cartridges and quality optics to make challenging, distant shots. However, not all brush-country hunting is a far-off affair. The close-range tactic of rattling was perfected by Texans.

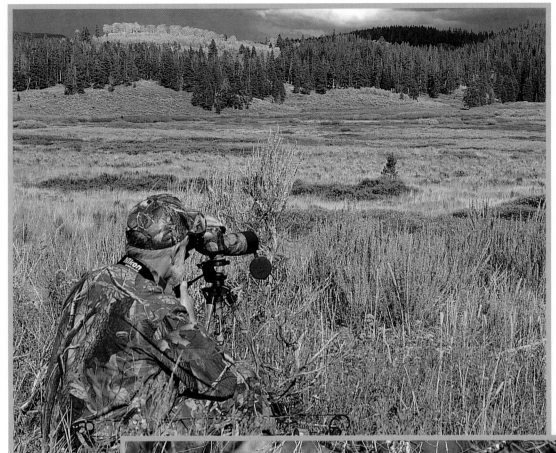

The mountains and plains of the West can show any hunter how important it is to be physically fit for the hunt.

The brush country of Texas has proven to be a fruitful hunting area of North America. Many Pope and Young and Boone and Crockett trophies have come from the area over the years.

The South

The South has abundant deer populations and deep-rooted hunting traditions. Excellent deer habitat and a warm climate allow some southern states to offer long hunting seasons and generous bag limits. Hunting terrain ranges from forested mountain ridges to semi-tropical swamps, but much of the hunting occurs in rural areas with a mix of agricultural and forested lands. In some areas, extensive private timberlands offer hunting opportunities.

In most southern states, finding places to hunt requires some legwork, because public hunting areas generally are limited. Many hunters choose to lease private land or join a hunting club to gain access. In recent years, increasing numbers of landowners and lessees have begun managing their property for

deer. This management often includes the development of food plots or whitetail habitat. Hunters on the property are encouraged to practice selective harvest, which typically is focused on achieving an adequate doe kill and not harvesting young bucks. The management intent is to balance the ratio of does and bucks, and to improve the herd's age structure. An effective management strategy may increase the number of mature bucks in the vicinity.

Southern whitetails generally are smaller than their northern kin. The rut begins later and lasts longer than in the North, though the peak rutting activity is generally less intense. Hunting from stands is a common tactic in the South and in better areas hunters may see several deer in the course of a day's hunt. To drive deer from dense cover, some southern states allow hunters to use dogs.

A permanent, elevated stand may be the perfect ticket to a successful hunt. It doesn't take the deer long to become accustomed to the new structure, and ignore it—even when you're inside.

Bucks, especially big bucks, are very secretive animals. Older bucks commonly live near people, yet they are almost never seen. We know bucks become more nocturnal as they age, so it's not too surprising that trophy bucks are so elusive. Some suggest that such big bucks leave an area when disturbance increases, but that seems unlikely—one study found that a density of 1 hunter per 10 acres did not force bucks to abandon their normal haunts.

A 1995 Texas study considered the way whitetail bucks react to human disturbance. The study showed that bucks were less flighty as they got older. Middle-aged bucks from 3½ to 4½ years old traveled farthest when spooked; bucks over 7½ years of age traveled the shortest distance. This research confirms what most experienced whitetail hunters already know—a big buck is secure in his home range. He's learned that slow, deliberate movements away from potential danger work better than a long, panic-stricken run.

Bucks that survive to old age are cagey about the bedding areas they select, too. In skimpy cover like the farm country of the Midwest, bucks may travel several miles from choice nighttime feeding areas to the dense cover where they bed down during the day. In the South's extensive timber plantations, good cover and browse are nearly always close together, so bucks don't have to travel as far between forage and secure bedding areas.

A pregnant doe eats for herself and her unborn fawn in the spring, so she often generally beds close to prime feeding areas and maximizes her chow time. For this reason, it's not unusual to see does in strips of cover near farming operations. Trophy bucks aren't as desperate for food and often prefer to bed as far away as possible from human disturbance. This may leave them far from the best feed. Some biologists suggest that this habit may have evolutionary value. The mature buck may leave the best feed to his does so that his offspring are born healthy and vigorous, preserving his genes in the next generation. As the summer progresses, a buck's antlers and body begin to demand more energy and he may move into prime feeding areas nearer the does.

Trophy bucks spend much of their time in impenetrable cover. These areas provide bucks with such dependable sanctuary that they often use them as bedding sites for months, even years. Often as small as 1 to 2 acres, these refuges provide the buck with the cover he needs to hide during the day and ready access to nearby feeding areas at night.

In the South, these hideouts are often in swamps. In the Northwest, they may be impenetrable willow thickets next to a major river, positioned so that prevailing winds allow safe ingress and egress. In the North, they may be thick conifer stands; hawthorn thickets; abandoned fields with dense tangles of sumac, prickly ash or aspen or a combination thereof. During the rut the trails to and from these bedding sites will be marked with many rubs. The bedding area itself will have some major rubs, perhaps a scrape and lots of deer pellets in a small area.

CHAPTER SIX

After the Hunt

et's assume you've been successful to this point in your deer hunt. You prepared in advance of the hunt by scouting, practicing with your firearm or bow and learning which techniques to use in your particular hunting area. Now you stand watching the spot where the deer was standing before you fired your weapon. What happens now?

Trailing Wounded Deer

Hunters may buy expensive equipment, travel great distances and spend countless hours hunting, only to lose a deer because they didn't know how to trail it after the shot.

The trailing process starts when you squeeze the trigger or release the arrow. Watch carefully to spot an entrance wound or protruding shaft. Deer hit in a vital area with a single, well-placed shot won't run far and are usually easy to recover. Remembering the details of the shot will help you find a deer that requires trailing.

Before trailing the deer, mark the location from which you shot. This way, you can easily find it again should you need to backtrack. Walk along the line your bullet or arrow traveled; if you find nicks or gouges in vegetation, your shot may have deflected enough to miss the deer.

Deer Behavior

As you shoot, watch the deer through your sights and study its reactions.

• A leg, rib or grazing shot usually makes a deer jump and run.

• A heart or lung shot may produce similar reactions, or the deer may show no immediate response, then bolt away at full speed. But it will seldom go more than 200 yards.

• A gut-shot deer often holds its tail down and hunches up as it runs.

• A brain or spinal-column shot will drop a deer in its tracks.

If you miss, the deer may stand still or take a few bounds and then wait to try to pinpoint any further sign or movement, giving you a chance to shoot again. Even if you don't get another shot, follow up your first one. Many a hunter has been surprised to find a dead deer just over the ridge after what he or she assumed was a sure miss.

If you hit the deer and it runs off, stay put—a few minutes for gun hunters, perhaps 60 for bowhunters. Many deer are lost because the hunter follows too quickly. Frantic, unplanned pursuits blot out tracks and blood sign that could lead you to the deer. Or you could spook the deer and cause it to run again.

Despite many claims to the contrary, you can't predict the behavior of wounded deer. It's not true that deer always run uphill, or go to water or run a straight course. Do your trailing based on the sign you find, not where you think the deer should go.

Some states allow the use of trailing dogs, which can be a great help in recovering wounded deer.

If the shot is a good one, the blood trail should lead you directly to the downed deer.

Hair and Blood Clues

Look for hair around the shot site. Lots of hair most likely means a grazing shot; only a little hair, a body shot. You'll find mostly brown hair if the shot was high; white if it was low. Noticing bone fragments, signifying a leg hit, can also be helpful.

Carefully studying blood at the scene of the shot can provide some valuable clues as to where the deer was hit and how you should proceed in tracking it. Don't disturb the site; mark it in case you need to reexamine it later.

Once you start trailing the deer, move as quickly as possible. If you proceed too slowly, the blood trail will dry and become much less obvious.

The blood trail is your best link to the deer. Always walk beside it, not on it, so you don't destroy clues. If you lose the blood trail, mark the last blood found, then look for overturned leaves, scuff marks or bent plants that may indicate the animal's direction. Deer tend to bleed more when they exert themselves, so you're more likely to pick up the blood trail where a deer has crossed a gully, ditch or fence. If you still can't pick up the blood trail, systematically search heavy cover nearby. Make every effort to retrieve a wounded animal before resuming the hunt, even if it takes the rest of the day.

It's really not possible to tell where a deer was hit by the color of the blood. Some people maintain that pink blood means a lung hit; dark blood, a liver hit, etc. But even blood experts can tell little about the wound's location based on color.

Don't jump to conclusions based on the first blood sign. The initial blood pattern may be misleading because any wound causes immediate surface bleeding. Look for one of the following patterns to develop:

• Fine droplets sprayed on both sides of the trail for the first 50 to 100 yards. Droplets may be several feet up on tree trunks and brush as well as on the ground. Small bubbles in the blood that burst when you touch them indicates a hit in the heart, lungs or large blood vessels in the neck.

The chances are good that you'll find your deer dead within 200 yards.

• Large splotches of blood at the spot where the animal was hit, turning to continuous drops that diminish within 100 to 200 yards. You may find some

This much hair near the shot site might indicate a grazing shot, probably low on the deer. It's quite possible the shot went under the belly and didn't hit any vital areas.

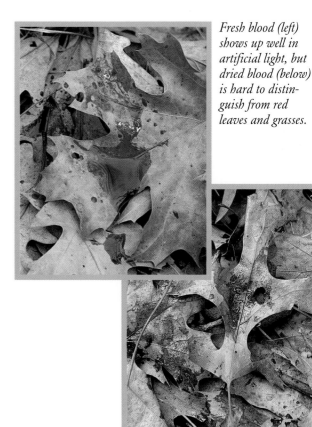

Fresh blood (left) shows up well in artificial light, but dried blood (below) is hard to distinguish from red leaves and grasses.

clots along the trail. Bleeding continues as long as the deer is moving but stops when the animal lies down. This pattern indicates a hit in the leg, back muscles or neck muscles, or rarely, in the body cavity. Eventually, these wounds will stop bleeding, so you'll have to trail the deer based on other clues.

• Blood trail is difficult to find at first, then large splotches appear between 20 and 50 yards. Blood sign steadily decreases until only scattered specks are found after 100 yards. This pattern is typical of gut-shot deer. Food particles in the area where you hit the deer and putrid-smelling blood confirm a gut shot.

The volume of blood circulating through the digestive system diminishes as the muscles of a moving deer demand more blood. This, together with clotting, explains why the blood trail thins out after about 50 yards.

Gut-shot deer are the most difficult to recover. If you suspect a gut shot, wait at least 2 hours before trailing, even if you fear the deer will spoil or rain will wash away the blood trail. When a deer beds, the blood flow to muscles decreases and flow to the gut increases. The deer will bleed to death in

its bed and will be found within 200 to 500 yards, if you don't chase it. But if you follow too soon and spook the deer from its bed, the trail will then have little, if any, blood.

Etiquette and Safety

No matter what type of trail you're following, ask your partners for help if you need it. Be sure to tell them exactly what to do. Be quiet, stay together and designate shooters for safety's sake. Someone should stay near the last blood spot and look ahead for the deer while the others search for more blood or tracks.

Always get permission before trailing onto any private land you don't have permission to hunt. Keep track of your location and use a compass or GPS unit—it's easy to get lost when you're concentrating on a blood trail.

Sooner or later you'll come upon the animal. If it's standing or bedded with its head up, shoot it again. Approach a downed deer slowly and quietly from behind, watching for signs of life. If it doesn't move, jab it with a stick. If it does, kill it with a rifle shot in the neck or an arrow in the chest cavity.

Blood in a pattern of fine spray (right) usually means a heart/lung hit. Big blotches changing to small drops (below) usually mean a muscle hit.

Make sure your deer is dead before moving in too close. A wounded whitetail can be dangerous.

Field-Dressing Whitetails

Proper care of wild game in the field ensures that the meat you bring home will be in prime condition for the table.

Immediate dressing drains blood and dissipates body heat. Always wear rubber gloves to protect yourself from any parasites or blood-borne diseases the animal may be carrying, and to make your cleanup easier.

Follow state regulations requiring evidence of the sex on the carcass. Where the law allows, attach the registration tag after field-dressing so it doesn't get torn off during the dressing procedure.

There are many ways to field-dress a deer. The following step-by-step instructions show one method we've found to get the job done.

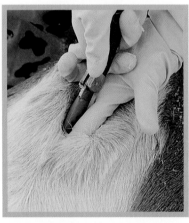

1. Locate the base of the breastbone by pressing on the center of the ribcage until you feel its end. Make a shallow cut that is long enough to insert the first two fingers of your left hand. Be careful not to puncture the intestines when cutting.

2. Form a V with the first two fingers of your left hand. Hold the knife between your fingers with the cutting edge up, as shown. (Your fingers prevent you from puncturing the intestines.) Cut through the abdominal wall to the pelvic area.

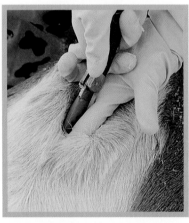

3. Separate the external reproductive organs of a buck from the abdominal wall, but do not cut them off completely. Remove the udder of a doe if she was still nursing. The milk sours rapidly, and could give the meat an unpleasant flavor.

4. Straddle the deer, facing its head. Unless you plan to mount the head, cut the skin from the base of the breastbone to the jaw, with the cutting edge of the knife up. If you plan to mount the head, see the tips on caping (page 116) and follow your taxidermist's instructions.

5. Brace your elbows against your legs, and use your knees for leverage. Cut through the center of the breastbone. If the deer is old or very large, you may need to use a game saw or small axe. If you have a helper, be sure he or she stands to the side in case the knife slips.

6. Slice between the hams to free a buck's urethra, or if you elect to split the pelvic bone on either a buck or doe. Make careful cuts around the urethra until it is freed to a point just above the anus. Be careful not to sever the urethra.

7. Cut around the anus; on a doe, the cut should also include the reproductive opening (above the anus). Free the rectum and urethra by loosening the connective tissue with your knife. Tie off the rectum and urethra with kitchen string (inset).

11. Remove liver after severing the attaching tubes. If you see spots, cysts or scarring on the liver (which could indicate parasites or disease), discard it. If the liver is clean, and you plan to eat it, place it in the plastic bag with the heart. Place on ice as soon as possible.

8. Free the windpipe and esophagus by cutting the connective tissue. Sever windpipe and esophagus at the jaw. Grasp them firmly and pull down, continuing to cut where necessary, until freed to the point where the windpipe branches out into the lungs.

12. Pull tied-off rectum and urethra underneath the pelvic bone and into the body cavity, unless you have split the pelvic bone. (If you have, this is unnecessary.) Roll the animal on its side so the entrails begin to spill out the side of the body cavity.

9. Hold ribcage open on one side. Cut the diaphragm, from the rib opening down to the backbone. Stay as close to the ribcage as possible; do not puncture the stomach. Repeat on other side so the cuts meet over the backbone.

13. Grasp the windpipe and esophagus firmly. Pull down and away from the animal's body. If the organs do not pull away freely, the diaphragm may still be partially attached. Scoop from both ends toward the middle to finish rolling out the entrails.

10. Remove the heart by severing the connecting blood vessels. Hold it upside down to drain excess blood. If you plan to eat the heart, place it in a plastic bag. Some hunters find it easier to remove the entrails first, then take the heart and liver from the gut pile.

14. Sponge cavity clean, and prop open with a stick. If the urinary tract or intestines have been severed, wash meat with snow or clean water. If you must leave the animal, drape it over brush or logs with the cavity down, or hang it from a tree to speed cooling.

TIPS FOR SAFELY HANDLING WILD GAME

Sources such as the Chronic Wasting Disease Alliance, Wisconsin Department of Natural Resources and other wildlife officials have suggested precautions for hunters field-dressing animals and handling deer in areas where CWD is found. The following are good tips to remember.

• Wear rubber or latex gloves when field-dressing carcasses.

• Avoid the use of saws. Do not cut through spine or skull.

• Bone out the meat from your animal.

• Remove all internal organs.

• Minimize the handling of brain, spinal cord, spleen and lymph nodes (lumps of tissue next to organs or in fat).

• Use equipment dedicated to field-dressing only; do not use household knives or utensils.

• Thoroughly clean knives and equipment, and sanitize by soaking in a mixture of equal parts chlorine bleach and water for 1 hour.

• If you will be using a professional processor, request that your animal be butchered individually and not combined with meat from other animals.

• Do not eat the eyes, brain, spinal cord, spleen, tonsils or lymph nodes of any deer.

• Do not eat any part of a deer that appears sick.

• If your deer is sampled for CWD testing, wait for test results before eating the meat.

Caping-Out Your Trophy

If you wish to mount the head of your deer, but have no caping experience, the job is best left to an expert. Though not particularly difficult, caping is time-consuming, and a slip of the knife could mean a less-than-perfect trophy.

Most taxidermists prefer that you bring the entire deer to them, so that they can skin and cape it to their own satisfaction.

If you cannot take the carcass to a taxidermist, the next-best option is to take the entire hide with head attached. To skin the deer; hang it by the hind legs and peel the hide down to the head before severing the neck. From brisket to head, the hide should be free of cuts. The taxidermist can then determine how much of the hide he needs for the mount and do the intricate work of skinning out the head himself.

Should circumstances dictate that you cape the deer yourself, follow the instructions on these pages. Also be sure to follow the precautions listed at left for safely handling wild game. Maintain a shaving edge on your knife and work slowly and carefully because any mistake means extra work for the taxidermist.

If you'll be hunting a few more days, hang the cape or hide with head attached in the shade where air can circulate freely. Never place it in any type of container. Trapped air will warm quickly, causing the hide to spoil. Once home, get it to a taxidermist immediately. If you can't, store the hide in a freezer.

1. *Make 45-degree cuts (dotted lines) beginning at the inside of the base of each antler. Where the two cuts join, cut straight back along the center of the head to the point where it meets the neck. Make sure your cuts are shallow, through the hide only.*

2. *Start cutting several inches behind the front leg (dotted line) and continue cutting all the way around the body. Make sure you don't angle your cut too far toward the head. If you do, the taxidermist may not have enough hide to work with.*

3. *Cut around each front leg just above the knee (dotted lines), then cut up the back of the leg to meet the cut around the body. Pull the hide steadily toward the head, freeing any meat or fat that sticks to the hide. Peel down to the base of the skull; sever the head from the neck.*

4. *Pry the skin away from the antler bases with a screwdriver or other blunt tool. Be sure to get all the hair around the bases. Cut the cartilage that connects the ears to the skull so the ears remain attached to the hide. The taxidermist will finish skinning the ears.*

5. *Skin around the eyes with great caution. This skin, particularly the eyelids, is extremely thin. You could easily cut through it when trying to free it from the skull, especially if your knife is dull. Eyelids are very difficult for a taxidermist to repair.*

6. *Free the tear glands at the lower-front corner of each eye. The glands are recessed, so it's important that you cut deep enough and scoop them out. Otherwise, you'll leave a patch of skin on the skull, making extra work for the taxidermist.*

7. *Pry the mouth open and cut along the gumline to free the upper and lower lips. Pull the cape over the head and, from the inside, cut the remaining tissue at the back of the jaws. Skin the nose from the inside to free the cape; remove any cartilage, fat or meat.*

8. *Saw the antlers from the skull by cutting straight down between the antler bases and the eye sockets to a point about 1½ inches below the antler bases. Beginning at the back of the skull, make a second cut (shown) to intersect with the first.*

Field-Judging Antlers

Whether you're specifically targeting trophy-class bucks or not, you must be able to quickly recognize a true trophy from a slightly smaller buck. Easier said than done, because fully mature bucks usually don't stand still for long. Some monster bucks may not expose themselves to human eyes for more than 60 seconds in their entire lives.

At the same time, he who acts hastily finds himself dragging the wrong buck out of the woods. A buck that looks wide and heavy from the front might have just a few short tines when viewed from the side.

Record Books

The most widely accepted scoring system for whitetails is that of the Boone and Crockett Club (B&C), official record keepers for all North American big game. To be eligible for the B&C record book, bucks must be found dead or taken in fair chase by either gun or bow. The Pope and Young Club (P&Y), which maintains records for animals shot with bow and arrow only, also uses the B&C scoring system.

Both clubs maintain records in typical and non-typical categories. In the typical category, the more closely the two antlers match, the better the net score. Under the scoring system for typicals, deductions are made for asymmetry, meaning that unbalanced racks don't score as well as perfectly balanced ones of the same general dimensions. The minimum net score for a buck to qualify as a B&C typical is 170 points; P&Y, 125 points.

Many hunters prefer the rough-and-ready character of non-typical racks with odd-shaped sticker points and drop tines. As far as these sportsmen are concerned, any antler the buck manages to grow atop its head is just fine. Under the B&C scoring system, non-typical antlers are scored the same as typicals, with the usual deductions for asymmetry, but all abnormal points are then added to the final score. Minimum entry score for a B&C non-typical is 195 points; P&Y, 150 points.

Two Boone and Crocket bucks. One, with a set of typical antlers measuring over 200 inches (left), has a different look than a non-typical with 21 points and an outside spread of about 37 inches (right). Both would be beautiful trophies.

This buck sports wide-sweeping antlers and a heavy body, two characteristics of a trophy-class deer. With a little practice, you'll train yourself to quickly count points and calculate things like tine length and main beam circumference.

Deer Anatomy

Estimating antler size in the field is done by comparing the features of the antlers against other anatomical features of known dimension.

For example, the ears of a mature buck are generally 6 to 8 inches long; the spread between the tips of the ears, 16 to 18 inches. The nose-to-eye distance on most mature bucks is 7 to 8 inches, and the circumference of the eye is about 4 inches.

Knowing these dimensions lets you estimate the pertinent antler measurements of the B&C scoring system: the length of the main beam and each tine; the circumference of the main beam, measured at the base and between the tines; and the inside spread between the antlers. But you'll need to do these calculations as quickly as possible; you often have little time to judge these measurements and add them for a rough estimate of the buck's score.

The best training for field-judging antlers is to study photographs and, more important, mounted heads of known score. Practice by studying mounted heads from different angles, estimating the antler measurements by comparing them to the anatomical features. Use a tape measure to check your guess.

Memorize how a 22-inch-wide rack looks from the front compared to an 18-inch rack. Notice how a long main beam reaches back, swings wide, then curls forward toward the deer's nose, while a shorter beam usually remains straight at the tips. If you find a set of antlers that curls in at the tips, measure them for beam length—you'll be surprised to discover these curved antlers are much longer than they first appear.

After a little practice, you'll soon develop a knack for estimating a buck's general score at a glance. That's the key for quickly and accurately field-judging live bucks.

Ear length is 6 to 8 inches (1). Use the ear for comparison when estimating the length of the tines and main beam. Ear spread measures 16 to 18 inches between tips (2). Use this distance to estimate the inside antler spread.

Nose-to-eye distance, usually 7 to 8 inches, can help you estimate the length of the main beam and tines (1). Eye circumference is about 4 inches (2). Use the eye for comparison when estimating antler circumference, or mass, near the base and between the next three tines.

Scoring Basics

It is relatively easy to learn how to estimate a buck's general score—for instance, a 110-class typical verses a 150. But if you're hoping to take a buck that qualifies for either record book, you'll need to learn how to score more precisely.

Here are five easy steps:

1. Count the tines on one antler, guess the length of each and add these measurements.

2. Estimate the length of the main beam, plus its circumference at the base and between the tines; add these numbers to your score.

3. Double this number, assuming the other antler is relatively symmetrical to the first.

4. Estimate the inside spread between the antlers and add this number to get the total rough score.

5. If time permits, you can subtract points for any broken or missing tines.

Practice Example

Let's assume you're stand hunting with a rifle and you see a deer trot through an opening in the brush. You see the rack—it's heavy, tall and wider than the distance between the tips of the ears. These features alone place it roughly in the 130- to 150-class, and if you sense the buck is about to bolt, you might take a shot based only on this glance.

But the buck is in no hurry. He stops, presenting himself broadside, and you quickly focus his head in your binoculars. You see three tall tines sticking up from the main beam, so he's probably a 10-pointer.

You can't yet see the brow tine, but the next tine up (the G-2 tine in the scoring system) looks about 2 inches longer than the ear (which you know is about 8 inches long), making this tine close to 10 inches. The next tine is shorter, about 6 inches; the third is about half as long as the ear; call it 4 inches. Add 10, 6 and 4 for 20 points. (You'll add in the length of the brow tine when the buck turns to expose it.)

You see that the main beam stretches forward to halfway between the buck's eye and nose and reaches pretty high above his head. You decide that the main beam looks to be about three times longer than the 8-inch eye-to-nose distance, giving you 24 inches. Add this number to the previous score, for a total of 44.

While waiting for the buck to present a front-on view, you can score the antler mass by estimating the circumference of the main beam. The base of the antler looks considerably larger than the circumference of the buck's eye, which is about 4 inches, so you guess the antler is about 6 inches around. That's thick! The beam stays thick past the first and second points before beginning to taper off, so you add 6 plus 6 plus 5 plus 4 to arrive at 21. Added to the previous 44 points, you've now scored a total of 65. Double this score for the other antler and you're already up to 130—and you haven't yet added in the spread between antlers or the length of the brow tines.

Finally the deer turns and looks right at you, revealing antlers that extend about 1 inch beyond the tip of each ear. You know the distance between the tips of his ears is about 18 inches, so that means the antler spread must be about 20 inches. You're up to 150 points. Now you see the brow tines; they are surprisingly short, only about 4 inches long. Double this number for 8 inches, and add this in for a total score of 158!

Do you take this buck? Although its score falls below Boone & Crockett minimums, this animal is a fantastic trophy. Ultimately, it's up to each hunter to set his or her own criteria for what qualifies as a "shooter."

Whitetail Conservation

Over the 300 years between the arrival of Columbus and the virtual colonization of the United States from coast to coast, whitetail numbers fluctuated repeatedly. Indian and white hunters killed large numbers for meat and hides to send to market. Settlers often depended heavily upon native game while they cleared the forest for their farms. When these farms would fail, as they often did, and the settlers would move even farther west, depleted deer populations rebounded temporarily as nature reclaimed the clearings, providing prime whitetail habitat. This cycle repeated itself many times in the settling of North America.

In the late 1800s, once the continent was laced with roads and railroads that could carry both settlers west and white-tailed deer parts to market, the extermination of the white-tailed deer began. Venison was a popular staple of city dwellers and could be found on the menu of many fine restaurants and for sale in markets. In order to feed this demand, market hunters took to the woods. At the same time, residents of burgeoning rural communities went afield to hunt whitetails. With no hunting seasons or bag limits, a growing human population took a heavy toll on not only white-tailed deer, but many other native species. Although this era's unregulated sport hunting contributed to the whitetail's decline, the larger blame can be laid upon an insatiable appetite for venison in the cities and a desire for the supple leather created from the deer's hide.

From a pre-Columbus population of somewhere between 23 and 33 million, the whitetail's numbers crashed to an estimated low of 350,000 to 500,000 by 1900. The pressure on white-tailed deer only diminished when they became so difficult to find that it was no longer profitable to go afield. In many parts of the U.S., whitetails were virtually extinct or only remnant populations remained.

Early hunter-conservationists grew alarmed and were instrumental in seeking laws to protect this highly esteemed and beautiful animal–the very root of wildlife management in this country. With the advent of controlled hunting seasons and bag limits, combined with this new science of wildlife management, whitetails climbed back from the brink of extinction.

Boy, how times have changed.

In many parts of North America, deer populations are so abundant, whitetails are considered a nuisance. The incidence of vehicle-deer collisions has increased dramatically in the last decade, and suburbanites, as they build their starter-mansions in what once was wild land, bump nose to nose with the adaptable whitetail and curse this animal's taste for their shrubbery.

It seems strange then to even talk about whitetail conservation. After all, they are doing quite well, aren't they?

Yes, they are, but there remains concern at several levels.

One such concern could be summed up by the term "habitat fragmentation." Whitetails do well in places where there are lots of edges and variety of habitats, so simply carving up habitat isn't always a problem. The concern arises when the use of this habitat is incompatible with hunting. Without hunting, whitetail populations skyrocket, and there is no other effective means of controlling them. Dot the woods with homes, though, and hunting becomes not only more difficult, but is often frowned upon, and sometimes outlawed.

This conflict is becoming more evident every day, and the only way to deal with it is for today's hunter-conservationist to become involved in land-use planning issues, so that unfragmented blocks of huntable habitat are preserved.

The second great concern arises from the privatization and commercialization of whitetails. North American hunting tradition and conservation is based on the simple principal that wildlife belongs to the state, not the individual on whose land it may spend time. This system has led to the creation of the most successful wildlife management system in the world. Without the public ownership of wildlife–whitetails included–the system will collapse because no one wants to pay for something from which they derive no benefit.

In several parts of the U.S., the whitetail is already semi-privatized, particularly in Texas. There, and elsewhere, "high fences" have gone up, enclosing large areas of land. Within are trapped the public's deer. It makes little difference that you couldn't have gotten permission to hunt this land anyway because without the fences, deer were free to leave that land (where you might then bag one), and to complete their natural cycle, which includes roaming to breed, thus benefiting the species, including those you harvest down the road.

With the advent of high fences, natural movement stops, and public ownership is essentially moot. In fact, many landowners perceive that they own the deer, and in the state of Texas, as this book was going to press, a bill had been introduced that indeed would make deer private property. Inside many of these high-fence compounds, individuals are also manipulating whitetail genetics for the sake of larger antlers.

Whitetails have also become a commodity to buy and sell, even over the Internet. Canned hunts for large-racked, semi-domesticated whitetails are offered in many parts of the country. An insult to both the animal and to our hunting traditions, these canned killings risk raising the ire of non-hunters, and casting all hunting in a very dim light.

Finally, there is the very real threat of disease, the most serious of which is known as chronic wasting disease (CWD).

Essentially the wild counterpart of the now infamous mad cow disease of Great Britain, CWD has now been found in wild deer in a half-dozen states. It is a particularly troubling disease, not only because it devastates the deer population, but because whitetails live in close proximity to people—and are also eaten by people—and there remains the real risk that, like mad cow disease, it may be transmissible to people.

Whitetails have been around a long time. No doubt, they'll be around a lot longer. They are remarkable creatures and seem well suited to adapt to most of the changes we throw at them.

But not all.

What nonhunters don't understand about those of us who hunt is that we love and respect our quarry. We appreciate the gift they are to us and value the time we spend in pursuit. But because they give us so much, we also owe it to the wildlife we hunt to work for the betterment of its habitat and health.

Not all hunters are conservationists. They should be. Consider joining an organization that works to preserve wild places and advance sound wildlife management practices. It is the least we can do for the animals we hunt.

INFORMATION SOURCES

The following are a few organizations and agencies that offer data concerning CWD, among other wildlife-related topics. Contact them for more information.

Boone and Crockett Club
406-542-1888
www.boone-crockett.org/news/news_cwd

Colorado Division of Wildlife
303-297-1192
http://wildlife.state.co.us

Chronic Wasting Disease Alliance
www.cwd-info.org

Kansas Department of Wildlife & Parks
620-342-0658
www.kdwp.state.ks.us

Minnesota Department of Natural Resources
651-296-6157
www.dnr.state.mn.us/mammals/deer/cwd.html

Montana Fish, Wildlife & Parks
406-751-4564
www.fwp.state.mt.us

Mule Deer Foundation
www.muledeer.org/cwd.htm
888-375-3337

Nebraska Game & Parks Commission
402-471-0641
www.ngpc.state.ne.us/homepage.html

New Mexico Department of Game and Fish
800-862-9310
www.gmfsh.state.nm.us

Oklahoma Conservation Commission
405-521-6787
www.okcc.state.ok.us

Pope and Young Club
507-867-4144
www.pope-young.org

Rocky Mountain Elk Foundation
800-225-5355
www.rmef.org

South Dakota Department of Game, Fish & Parks
605-394-2391
www.state.sd.us/gfp

The Wildlife Management Institute
202-371-1808

Wisconsin Department of Natural Resources
608-266-2621
www.dnr.state.wi.us

Whitetails Unlimited
800-274-5471
www.whitetailsunlimited.org

Wyoming Game and Fish Department
307-745-4046
http://gf.state.wy.us

Alberta Sustainable Resource Development
780-944-0313
http://www3.gov.ab.ca/srd/fw/index.html

Saskatchewan Environment & Resources
800-567-4224
www.serm.gov.sk.ca/fishwild/CWD-survey.htm

Index

Contributing Photographers & Manufacturers

(Note: T=Top, C=Center, B=Bottom, L=Left, R=Right, I=Inset)

PHOTOGRAPHERS

Charles J. Alsheimer
CharlesAlsheimer.com
© *Charles J. Alsheimer: pp. 3R, 15, 17, 28, 33, 52, 56, 67L, 76BL, 76BC, 76BR*

Mike Barlow
MikeBarlow.com
© *Mike Barlow: pp. 12TI, 76CL, 76CR, 106, 120both*

Denver Bryan
DenverBryan.com
© *Denver Bryan: back cover TL, p. 100*

Dembinsky Photo Associates
Owosso, MI
© *Bill Lea: p. 10T*
© *Dominique Braud: p. 31BR*

John R. Ford
Thorp, WI
© *John R. Ford: front cover, pp. 3L, 20, 32, 46T, 76T, 76CC*

Michael H. Francis
Billings, MT
© *Michael H. Francis: pp. 4, 9B, 16, 19*

Herndon's Photojournalism
Brownstown, IN
© *Brad Herndon: pp. 58T, 59, 65, 95, 102, 110*
© *Carol Herndon: pp. 58B, 66L, 66TR, 107T*

Tes Randle Jolly
Tuskegee, AL
© *Tes Randle Jolly: p. 108*

Donald M. Jones
Troy, MT
© *Donald M. Jones: back cover CR, pp. 10I, 12B, 21B, 22R, 27, 29, 31, 38T, 42, 62, 66BR, 71L, 72B, 86, 89, 94*

Bill Kinney
BillKinney.com
© *Bill Kinney: pp. 6, 8BL, 8BR, 13, 14, 23all, 31TR, 35, 38B, 46B, 105, 109, 118, 119both*

Lon E. Lauber
LonLauber.com
© *Lon E. Lauber: pp. 46B, 60TL, 68, 80L, 93T, 107B*

Bill Lea
BillLea.com
© *Bill Lea: back cover BR, pp. 10B, 11T, 11B, 18, 20I, 21T, 22L, 26, 31TL, 37TL, 37TR*

Bill Marchel
BillMarchel.com
© *Bill Marchel: pp. 3C, 12T, 36-37, 40, 67C, 67R, 93BL, 93BR, 104*

Mark Raycroft
Trenton, Ontario, Canada
© *Mark Raycroft: pp. 24, 31BL, 39, 87I, 103*

MANUFACTURERS

Barrie Archery, LLC
P.O. Box 482
Waseca, MN 56093
507-835-3859
507-835-5097
www.rockymtbroadheads.com

Browning
One Browning Place
Morgan, UT 84050
800-333-3504
801-876-3331
www.browning.com

Cabela's, Inc.
One Cabela Drive
Sidney, NE 69160
800-237-4444
800-496-6329
www.cabelas.com

Carl Zeiss Sports Optics
13005 N. Kingston Ave.
Chester, VA 23836
800-441-3005
804-530-8481
www.zeiss.com/sports

Gerber Legendary Blades
P.O. Box 23088
Portland, OR 97281
800-950-6161
www.gerberblades.com

HHA Sports
7222 Townline Road
Wisconsin Rapids, WI 54494
800-548-7812
www.hhasports.com

Hunter's Specialties
6000 Huntington Court NE
Cedar Rapids, IA 52402
319-395-0321
319-395-0326
www.hunterspec.com

Primos Hunting Calls, Inc.
604 First Street
Flora, MS 39071
601-879-9323
601-879-9324
www.primos.com

Scent-Lok
1731 Wierengo Drive
Muskegon, MI 49442
800-315-5799
231-767-2824
www.scentlok.com

Sightron, Inc.
100 Jeffrey Way, Suite A
Youngsville, NC 27596
919-562-3000
919-562-7129
www.sightron.com

Tink's
P.O. Box 244
Madison, GA 30650
800-713-7278
706-342-8993
www.tinks69.com

Creative Publishing international

is your complete source of How-to information for the Outdoorsman.

Available Outdoor Titles:

Hunting Books
- Advanced Turkey Hunting
- Advanced Whitetail Hunting
- Bowhunting Equipment & Skills
- The Complete Guide to Hunting
- Dog Training
- Duck Hunting
- Elk Hunting
- Hunting Record-Book Bucks
- Mule Deer Hunting
- Muzzleloading
- Pronghorn Hunting
- Whitetail Hunting
- Whitetail Techniques & Tactics
- Wild Turkey

Fishing Books
- Advanced Bass Fishing
- The Art of Freshwater Fishing
- The Complete Guide to
  Freshwater Fishing
- Fishing for Catfish

- Fishing Rivers & Streams
- Fishing Tips & Tricks
- Fishing with Artificial Lures
- Inshore Salt Water Fishing
- Kids Gone Fishin'
- Largemouth Bass
- Modern Methods of Ice Fishing
- Northern Pike & Muskie
- Offshore Salt Water Fishing
- Panfish
- Salt Water Fishing Tactics
- Smallmouth Bass
- Striped Bass Fishing: Salt Water
  Strategies
- Successful Walleye Fishing
- Trout

Fly Fishing Books
- The Art of Fly Tying
- The Art of Fly Tying – CD ROM
- Fishing Dry Flies – Surface
  Presentations for Trout in Streams

- Fishing Nymphs, Wet Flies &
  Streamers – Subsurface Techniques
  for Trout in Streams
- Fly-Fishing Equipment & Skills
- Fly Fishing for Trout in Streams
- Fly Fishing for Beginners
- Fly-Tying Techniques & Patterns

Cookbooks
- America's Favorite Fish Recipes
- America's Favorite Wild Game
  Recipes
- Babe & Kris Winkleman's
  Great Fish & Game Recipes
- Cooking Wild in Kate's Camp
- Cooking Wild in Kate's Kitchen
- Dressing & Cooking Wild Game
- Game Bird Cookery
- The New Cleaning & Cooking Fish
- Preparing Fish & Wild Game
- The Saltwater Cookbook
- Venison Cookery

To purchase these or other Creative Publishing international titles,
contact your local bookseller, or visit our web site at
www.creativepub.com

The Complete
FLY FISHERMAN™